Inspirations
of the Heart

Jacquelyn Scott, MHP

authorHOUSE®

AuthorHouse™
1663 Liberty Drive
Bloomington, IN 47403
www.authorhouse.com
Phone: 1 (800) 839-8640

Published by AuthorHouse 01/27/2017

ISBN: 978-1-5246-4786-5 (sc)
ISBN: 978-1-5246-4784-1 (hc)
ISBN: 978-1-5246-4785-8 (e)

Library of Congress Control Number: 2016918001

Print information available on the last page.

Table of Contents

4. God is Healing

5. God is Peace

Dedicated to my loving husband and children.

"I don't think Jesus is real, I *know* he is real."

– O. M. S., at five-years-old

Acknowledgements

I would like to take a moment to thank all who have helped to make the vision of this book become a reality. First, and foremost, I thank the Lord for His constant provision, blessings, and guidance throughout the entirety of this venture. His loving grace has made it possible for this book to come to fruition.

I thank my husband, Brad, whose constant support and patience has given me the freedom and courage to pursue my passion for faith-filled learning and writing. He patiently and attentively listened as I bounced countless ideas off of him during the development and creation of this book. He tirelessly read through numerous drafts of my personal writings, all the while helping me to pinpoint the purpose and vision for this book. I am forever grateful for all of his loving support.

I thank Marisa Deshaies whose keen editorial eye and expertise helped many story contributors, including myself, further develop their own line of vision for writing their stories.

I thank my lawyer who provided ample guidance and support throughout the story contributor recruitment process. His advice and expertise were invaluable and I greatly appreciate the time that he generously gave towards the initial phase of this project.

I extend my gratitude towards Msgr. J. H. for providing the resources needed to seek story contributor interest from his parish. His support opened many doors to the progression of the book as well as led to the recruitment of several story contributors. I go on to thank the many parishes within the Diocese of Wilmington, Delaware for their assistance in story contributor recruitment. Furthermore, I am so grateful to Msgr. J. H. and M. A. R. for providing their support and insight towards the final manuscript as I prepared to seek publication.

I also thank my dad, Carl Breerwood, for his amazing support as I pursued publication. Jesus had graciously answered a special intention of mine through the generosity of my father. Thank you, Jesus.

Finally, I would like to say an immense thank you to all of the individuals who contributed their personal stories of faith to this book.

Without them, this book would not be complete. Their openness to sharing the personal, and often very private, moments of their journeys of faith is a beautiful gift that they have given to all who read this book. I am honored to have the privilege of sharing each and every one of their stories. I can honestly say that their stories of faith have personally inspired me in numerous ways, which in turn, encouraged me to continue moving forward with this project, to see it through to the very end. Thank you!

Jacquelyn Scott, MHP

Introduction

The creation of this book was inspired by a personal journey of healing and self-discovery after a very challenging time in my life. This journey that I embarked upon deepened my understanding of the power of prayer, faith, and God's love in the obtainment of healing and peace. During and following this time of personal discovery, I was introduced to the beautiful and powerful stories of others who too had experienced the power of God's love.

My own life-experiences, coupled with numerous personal accounts of others, lead me to believe every person is presented with invaluable opportunities to know God. Some of these opportunities may transpire through random events, tragic experiences, or simple encounters with others. Whatever the catalyst may be, people have been led through personal experiences to find or renew their faith in God.

This book, therefore, is a collection of beautiful and inspiring stories that were written by individuals who have encountered God in the simple—yet, very real—setting of everyday life. These people have the courage and desire to share with you the goodness and love of God through their own testaments of how God's grace has brought peace, hope, and love into their lives, ultimately strengthening their own faith *in* and relationship *with* Him. These lived-experiences invite you to see and understand that God is indeed real; He is present, merciful, and all-loving; and He actively works in each of our lives when we open our hearts to Him.

"I prayed to the Lord, and he answered me; he freed me from all my fears. The oppressed look to him and are glad; they will never be disappointed. The helpless call to him, and he answers; he saves them from all their troubles. His angel guards those who honor the Lord and rescues them from danger. Find out for yourself how good the Lord is. Happy are those who find safety with him." (Psalm 34:4-8 Good News Translation [GNT])

1

God is Love

"God bestows His blessings without discrimination…"

– F. F. Bruce

A Friend Loves at all Times

I was a sophomore in college when I awoke one morning from a dream about a high school friend of mine, Laura Ann. She and I had once been the best of friends, but by the time college came around, we rarely kept in touch. An energetic, outgoing, upbeat person who was a one-of-a-kind friend, Laura Ann befriended me the first week of our freshman year of high school. As the new girl in school, I was grateful for her friendly introduction, which quickly blossomed into a beautiful kinship.

However, the challenges of high-school-life, such as boys, cliques, and extracurricular activities, tested my relationship with Laura Ann, causing us to slowly drift our own separate ways. Though our friendship became distant, Laura Ann always found a way to reach out to me, letting me know that she still considered me as her friend. Immature in my ways of maintaining a friendship, I was not fully receptive to her kind gestures and did not always reach back.

During our junior year of high school two major changes took place that directly affected our friendship. The first change was that I transferred high schools shortly after the start of the school year. The opportunity to attend the private Catholic high school that I had wanted to attend since freshman year was presented to me, and I jumped on it. The Catholic-school-system that I grew up with was so different than the public school I currently attended and, frankly, I missed it. However, the timing of the transfer wasn't perfect because around that same time, the second change took place: Laura Ann was diagnosed with Ewing's Sarcoma, a form of bone cancer. Though our friendship was slipping away, I still cared tremendously for Laura Ann, and the news of her cancer broke my heart. It seemed so unfair that such a horrible thing was happening to a young and wonderful person. No one could make sense of this tragic news, but true to her good nature, Laura Ann made the best out of this surreal situation and continued to radiate positivity and love.

Despite the physical and emotional distance between us, she never gave up on me. I wasn't sure why she continued to reach out to me because I definitely did not deserve her efforts. But, Laura Ann was different than most people: God gifted her with a genuine heart, one which she used to the fullest by always placing others before herself, including me. Her compassion towards our withered friendship was evident when she presented me with a small ornamental gift months after her diagnosis. On this gift there was a picture of two girls standing close to one another with a short proverb painted above their heads: "A friend loves at all times…" (17:17). God used this moment to teach me one of His greatest lessons: "[…] As I have loved you, so you must love one another" (John 13:34 GNT). Unfortunately, it would take years for His message to sink in because at that point in time I was not brave enough to face the reality of Laura Ann's condition. I thought if I kept my distance from her then the pain that I felt for her would remain distant. I was selfish.

Well, in this dream I alluded to, Laura Ann had lost her battle with cancer and passed away. I awoke with such a saddened feeling in my heart because even though Laura Ann and I grew apart, I still felt close to her. Through this dream I realized how much I missed her friendship. I felt guilty that I had pushed her away because I truly cared about her. With all of these feelings, I took a moment to reflect upon my experiences in that dream. As I lay there awake in my dorm room thinking about Laura Ann, my cell-phone rang. I looked at my phone and saw that it was my mom calling. I instinctively knew what she was going to tell me: Laura Ann had died.

My mom found out the news of Laura Ann the morning after she passed because my mom and Laura Ann's mom were going to be holding a rosary party for Laura Ann that afternoon. They had been holding the rosary parties for Laura Ann's healing once a month for about a year or so. My mom had mentioned the idea to Laura Ann's mom one time at a high school football game because my extended family had gotten together to pray the rosary for the healing of a cousin who had cancer. Since we took the time to pray all three mysteries of the rosary during these get-togethers, food and refreshments were served following the completion of each mystery. These prayerful get-togethers soon became known as "rosary parties". After getting together on multiple occasions to pray for the miracle of my cousin's healing from cancer, our prayers were answered; he was completely healed and cancer-free.

Through this conversation between Laura Ann's mom and my mom, Laura Ann's mom said she wanted a miracle for her daughter. So she hosted the parties while my mom led the rosary. Family and friends who were of all faiths came together to pray the rosary for the miracle of Laura Ann's healing. It was a beautiful thing. I wasn't always able to attend the parties because I was away at college for many of them, but the times that I did attend I was always moved by the amount of love, tears, and humility that were present during the rosaries that were prayed.

Although the intention was not answered in the way we had all expected, God answered all of our prayers in amazing and different ways, ways in which we never would have known if we had not gone to Him and asked for His help. And, when the time came for God to call Laura Ann home to Him, her mom said that those last three years of Laura Ann's life were the best years they had together and, amazingly, her mom did not have bitterness in her heart for the fact that Laura Ann was not healed of her cancer. The strength, peace, and closeness that Laura Ann and her family were given during that time were the answers to all of the prayers.

Stunned with the timing and reality of the news, I quietly thanked my mom for the call and hung up the phone. I laid my head back down on the pillow and pulled the covers over my head. Trying to remain as quiet as possible so I wouldn't wake my roommate, I muffled my cries into the pillow as I thought about the sad loss of someone so beautiful inside and out. I didn't understand why someone who was so genuine, so pure of heart, suffered so intensely just to be robbed of her life. Then, I thought about Jesus—He too had innocently suffered and was unjustly taken from this earth.

This thought of Jesus' suffering led me back to a time when my mom and I talked about the movie, *The Passion*, which so powerfully presented the horrific suffering Jesus endured for the sake of our human race. As we talked, my mom told me about Laura Ann's reaction to the movie after she had seen it with her mom. Laura Ann apparently turned to her mom and said, "What I am going through is *nothing* compared to what Jesus went through." I was amazed at her humble response and deeply touched by her ability to set aside her own suffering with cancer in acknowledgement of the tremendous sacrifice Jesus made for our salvation.

After receiving the tragic news of Laura Ann's passing, I contacted my professors informing them that I would be missing class to attend the funeral. Unsurprisingly, huge crowds of people gathered at both the viewing and funeral for Laura Ann. There was a collective desire for people, young and old alike, to come together in support of her family as well as to pay their respects to a person who, in such a short amount of time, touched the lives of so many people. Our presence was a way for us to say, "thank you" to Laura Ann for sharing her love with the world around her. It was a beautiful service, and I only wished my heart was able to grieve the loss of her without the guilt of a lost friendship compounding the pain.

Some time passed, and I continued to think about her. I still carried around guilt for not being there for her during her struggle with cancer, a time when a true friend would have stuck by her side. I felt guilty for allowing trivial differences and my transfer to a new high school to serve as excuses for a lost friendship. Now I would never be able to set things right with Laura Ann because she was gone. I knew in my heart that I longed for forgiveness that I didn't believe I deserved.

One weekend, several months following the funeral, I was home from college and decided to take a walk around the neighborhood. I found myself standing at Laura Ann's gravesite in the cemetery that was in walking distance of my parents' house. For a while I just stood there and looked around, taking everything in. Then, to my direct left, I noticed an angel chime hanging from a tree. I smiled as I saw it because it reminded me of her: a being who carries out God's work—a work of love.

After standing for a while, just breathing and listening to the quiet surroundings, the guilt I carried finally surfaced, and I fell to my knees. I cried as I felt the ground beneath me. I started talking out loud as the tears rolled down my face. I told Laura Ann that I was sorry for allowing petty things to get in the way of a wonderful friendship we once shared.

And, more importantly, I apologized for not being there for her during a time when she needed a friend the most.

After I finished saying the things I had wanted to say for such a long time, I heard the sweet sound of the angel chimes ringing. I looked around to find that the branches of the nearby trees remained completely still, including the tree from which the chimes hung; there was no breeze. Just then, I felt a peace engulf my heart—as if it was hugging me—and I smiled. I believe that Laura Ann had heard me and wanted me to know that everything is okay between us. I was forgiven. God allowed me to experience this blessing; He let me receive closure with someone who I cared so deeply about because He knew how much it meant to me. God's compassion is an overwhelmingly beautiful gift that He offers to every single one of us, even when we think we don't deserve it.

I still dream about her from time to time, but they are good and happy dreams that reflect a friendship we share, not in past form, but in the present. My subconscious is revealing the peace that I now hold in my heart. And when I think about her, I thank God for gifting the world with His precious Laura Ann.

Although my relationship with Laura Ann lasted only a couple of years, God granted her the grace to teach me an invaluable lesson that will last for a lifetime: *a friend loves at all times.* Through her example, I learned that you should never give up on loving someone no matter what the differences may be because we are all called to love just as God loves us—unconditionally.

Jacquelyn Scott

Our Three Moms

I grew up in a loving family with three boys—my fraternal twin, Michael, my older brother, Jeff, and me. Our parents split when Michael and I were just a few years away from entering our teens. Yet, we always knew that despite our parents' differences, they loved us unconditionally and worked incredibly hard to provide for and raise us in the best way they possibly could. We felt we lacked nothing of life's opportunities.

Our mother, Judy, is Canadian of Polish and Ukrainian descent; our father, Jim, is American, originally from South Carolina and served in the U.S. Air Force. They met while our dad was stationed at the Pentagon in Washington, D.C., and our mother was visiting a friend in Virginia. After getting married, our parents eventually moved to Canada with my brothers and me when I was almost two-years-old. Being born in the United States yet growing up in Canada, we had the privilege of dual citizenship. After they divorced, my brothers and I lived with our mother and would visit our father every second weekend. Both parents eventually remarried. Often my friends would comment on how much I looked like my father, which was fascinating considering that Michael and I didn't come into our parents' lives until we were about five-weeks-old—we were adopted.

For years I was interested in discovering who my biological parents were. Not only to satisfy thirty years of curiosity with respect to where my smile and my eyes came from, but also because I was interested in potentially meeting additional siblings and finding out their occupations. Our mother had her hands full with three boys, so the possibility of having a sister was also exciting. Michael was interested in the possibility and supportive of my endeavor in that he agreed to split the cost equally if I would spearhead the search.

Our mother told Michael and me how we were adopted through Catholic Charities in Washington D.C., and how much of a blessing we were as she had always wanted twins. We were the first set of twins to come through that office in seventeen years, so after some digging, it wasn't too hard for me to locate the particular office that had our file.

The social worker whom I spoke with, Roslyn, sent me the paperwork to start the process for identifying our biological parents and explained that there were two steps. The first step involved a background check and payment of a small fee, after which the agency would gather and then summarize all the information provided at the time of our adoption. The second was to petition the court to break the seal of adoption and start a search.

Among the paperwork was a statutory declaration that I needed to swear before a notary in order to verify my identity. In addition to being a driven and passionate individual, I can also be one of the world's worst procrastinators, and this indeed was the case in getting the statutory declaration sworn. Months went by until almost a year had passed, at which point I had misplaced the documents altogether. I don't remember exactly what sparked the motivation inside of me again, but I eventually got in touch with Roslyn and she re-sent the paperwork to me. This time I connected with a lawyer in Toronto who signed the document and I sent it, along with the rest of the forms and payment, back to Washington, D.C. Roslyn called me and said that she had received my paperwork, and mentioned that she was going on vacation for a week, but ensured me we would receive our background information in the mail within a month. However, just one week later, on Easter Monday, I received a call from Roslyn in which she declared, "Brian you're not going to believe this, but an hour ago I was on the phone with your birth mother." How was that possible? I couldn't believe it!

She explained that a woman had called the office saying that she had reason to believe her twins might try to get in touch with her. The woman said she didn't know how or when, but wanted Roslyn to have it on record that if we did try to contact her through Catholic Charities, she would be amenable to being put in touch with us.

Roslyn told the woman on the phone that she did currently have a client who was a twin, but wasn't legally allowed to disclose whether this client was one of *her* twins (even though she knew by the woman's description that Michael and I were most likely her sons). From the other end of the line the woman could sense Roslyn's astonishment after reviewing the file with the information that the woman provided. Roslyn told the woman that she would get back to her in a few days (which would end up turning into a few months).

It was obvious at this point that we could skip the background check, as we would be able to learn everything about our adoption from our biological mother herself. The cost of the second step, which required petitioning the court to break the seal of adoption, was now cut in half since we could bypass most of the red tape of the search. Roslyn explained that she was still legally required to attempt to get in touch with our biological father before she could connect us with our mother, as they were not married and both parties needed to give consent. There was also further paperwork that needed to be done in order to break the seal of adoption, which included an interview with a counselor to confirm we were emotionally capable of handling any scenario that could unfold.

During Memorial Day weekend of May 2009 I made a trip to Alexandria, Virginia to visit my godparents and also drove another hour into Fredericksburg to visit friends. I got in touch with Roslyn and arranged to visit her in-person at the office in Washington, D.C on my way home to conduct the remaining interview.

About a month later (on a Wednesday), Roslyn called and informed me that our biological father had passed away one year earlier. She also told me that our birth mother's name was Lucille—or Lucy for short—and gave me her home and cell phone numbers. I was told that Lucy was waiting for me to initiate contact with her directly. Needless to say, I was very excited, but also very nervous! I planned to wait until I could devote enough time towards a proper conversation, and two days later on a Friday evening after work, I finally decided to call her.

I dialed her home number and a woman with a sweet, higher-pitched voice answered. I said, "Hello, is this Lucy?" When she replied yes, I somewhat awkwardly said, "Hi Lucy, this is Brian, your twin son calling from Canada". She replied, somewhat awkwardly herself, "Oh, yes, hello ... wow ... so, what (slight pause) prompted you to try and get in touch with me?" And from there the conversation eased into an incredible and enlightening chat between the two of us. At one point during our conversation I was standing in my bedroom looking into the mirror, and in an overwhelming jolt of excitement and elation, I jumped up and down and clenched my fists as if to silently scream "Yes!!!" The gap I felt for thirty-one years was slowly starting to fill in with answers. We talked for an hour-and-a-half, and Lucy explained a lot during that conversation, most importantly how she met Eric, our biological father. She spoke of the heart-wrenching difficulty in giving us up for adoption, and how she wanted to give us the gift of being raised in a family that had the strong parental unit of both a mother and a father. I learned that Lucy had already had two children, Josh and Tara, who were very young at the time when she gave us up for adoption. I was excited to have just gained two half-siblings, and one of whom was a sister! As it turned out, Lucy herself was the second-oldest of nine siblings, which meant we had around forty cousins. Talk about a huge family!

During the entire conversation I was taking notes and jotting down as much as I could—there was so much information and history to take in. We emailed each other pictures of ourselves, and it was neat to hear the surprise in her voice as she opened the picture of me. She was as taken back at seeing the family resemblance in me as I was in seeing my resemblance to her. We also discovered that as babies she had given us names, knowing full well that whomever would adopt us would want to claim the task of naming us themselves. She named me Gabriel Addison, after the angel Gabriel who visited Mary in the New Testament, and Addison for the old English name that means "son of Adam." The name she gave Michael was Rocco Tobias, after her father Rocco. "Tobias" is a Hebrew biblical name meaning, "Yahweh is good". We learned that Lucy didn't even know she was carrying twins until we were born! Michael was born four minutes after I was, so needless to say, he was a pleasant surprise—a gift from God!

We eventually ended the conversation and Lucy asked if I would be comfortable with her daughter Tara (my half-sister) calling me. I said yes, of course! And Lucy eventually asked us if our mother, Judy, would be okay with speaking to her over the phone. She wanted to thank our mother for being the one to adopt us and raise us. Our mom was okay with this, and it turned out that she and Lucy had a lot in common. They shared a mutual gratitude and respect toward each other and were in awe of how clever our Lord was in connecting their two families back in 1978 and then again thirty-one years later. The two would eventually develop a unique friendship.

A few days later, Michael called Lucy, and left a voicemail and comically stating, "It's been a while, and would love to catch up!" After a brief game of phone-tag, Michael and Lucy too had an exciting first chat, which also lasted an hour-and-a-half.

Furthermore, Lucy made an effort to get in touch with members of our biological father's side of the family. Though Eric had passed away from esophageal cancer less than a year earlier, we discovered that through him we had an older half-sister, Melissa, and two younger half-siblings, Savannah and Christian, in addition to another handful of cousins, as Eric had six siblings. Melissa had grown up knowing about us, but Savannah and Christian had no idea that we existed. They were amazed when Melissa told them that their father once had twin sons and that they had now re-connected with the family.

Though Michael and I always suspected as we were growing up that we had other siblings, I didn't realize that there would be five of them! We went from having two siblings to seven in the blink of an eye.

It was inevitable that Michael and I would want to arrange a trip to Maryland and Virginia to meet Lucy and everyone else in the family. Our mother (Judy) had been supportive of our pursuit from the outset; however, we noticed there were times when she seemed to have mixed emotions about the whole situation. What would this mean for her? How would Michael and I react, and would meeting our birth family impact our relationship with our own mother? These were natural questions any mother would ask. Michael and I reassured her that this meeting, along with our undeniable excitement, would in no way lessen the love we had for her—our mom! We felt that it would make our bond even stronger through appreciation and gratitude. We gave the same reassurance to our father, Jim, who had been re-married for over twenty-four years to his loving wife Martha—our stepmother. They were nothing but supportive in our quest to discover our birth family. Martha was like a second mother to us, as she had been in our lives since we became teenagers. She often jokingly referred to herself as "Mom #3", because chronologically she was the third mom. We were sure to keep them both in the loop as all of these events were unfolding.

As that summer was very busy, we decided that the fall would be a better time for the trip, so we started planning for a trip in October of 2009. We wanted our mom to share the experience of this highly anticipated reunion, so in October the three of us flew to Baltimore and met Lucy, Josh, Tara, and their kids for the very first time. When we saw them at the airport we set our luggage down and I approached Lucy. I was the first to give her a big, warm embrace.

It was as much a soothing feeling as it was peculiar. I was embracing the woman who gave birth to me, who I was meeting for the first time as an adult. And though it wasn't the exact same familiar feeling as hugging my mom, I could no doubt feel her strong motherly love in that hug. Michael then had his moment with Lucy in an equally warm and heartfelt greeting. Finally, mother greeted mother, and both Michael and I witnessed the genuine smiles on their faces. We all made our introductions and were eventually on our way.

During that first weekend of the trip a "Cousin's Night Out" was arranged, where we met a lot of our family on Lucy's side while experiencing some of the Annapolis nightlife. Our mom also arranged a phone-call between Lucy and Martha, so that Lucy could meet our "other mother" too.

At the end of the weekend, after we had met most of Lucy's side of the family, our mother went to stay with good friends of hers, our godparents Rosemary and John, who lived in Alexandria, Virginia. Our siblings on Eric's side of the family also lived in Virginia, so midway through the week Michael and I joined our mom and our godparents in Alexandria. It was at their house that we first met our other siblings—Melissa, Savannah, and Christian—when they dropped by for the first time. After we embraced them and made our introductions, the group of five siblings went out for dinner at a nearby restaurant called Bonefish Grill where Eric had often taken them. We discovered that during many of Eric's later years, he lived in a house in Alexandria that was only a five-minute walk from our godparents' house! It was astonishing to think that during previous visits to Alexandria we could have passed Eric in the street without even realizing it.

The rest of our ten-day-trip was spent going back and forth equally between both sides of the family, and we soaked up the stories of our family history like a sponge. We got to know our biological father through many diverse pictures, videos and stories from those closest to him. One of the most fascinating things about meeting Lucy and seeing so many pictures of Eric was being able to recognize my physical features in theirs. This was something almost everyone grows up knowing or taking for granted, and I was discovering it for the first time at thirty-one! Michael excitedly did the same. Many of our biological cousins agreed that, while I resembled more of Eric's side of the family, Michael took after Lucy's.

This truly was the trip of a lifetime. When describing our whole experience to friends and acquaintances back at home, Michael often mentioned that not everyone who is adopted is interested in finding their biological family. And not everyone who truly is interested gets the chance to do so. And further, not everyone who chooses to is fortunate enough to discover their new-found family connections are even more welcoming and positive than they could have ever anticipated. We happened to be two of the fortunate ones.

At the time of our discovery I was working for Breakfast Television—a prominent Toronto morning show—and when I returned, the host of the show, TV personality Kevin Frankish, thought it would be great for my brother and me to share our incredible story during one of the live on-air segments. A few weeks later, we went on the show while Lucy telephoned in from Annapolis to share her perspective along with ours on live television.

We stayed in touch with our new-found family, and two months later it was our turn to host, as seven of them—five siblings and two cousins—made their first trip to Toronto to ring in the New Year with Michael and me.

In hindsight, I cannot help but wonder whether we would have had a chance to meet our biological father before he passed away if I hadn't initially taken so long to get the paperwork signed and put the search into motion. Maybe so, or maybe not—considering how long it would normally take to get through so much red tape. Either way I trust that God had it all planned out and that the Holy Spirit moved my heart when it needed to be stirred.

Another interesting perspective about the timing of everything is that Eric's side of the family had suffered three major losses during the previous year. They had lost our grandmother, Irma, to old age in June of 2008 (she was ninety), one of our cousins, Matthew, to a brain tumor in July (he was around our age), and our father, Eric to cancer in September (he had just turned sixty-two in August). When Eric's sister—our Aunt Cheryl—called Melissa to share the news of Michael and me, Melissa was so excited that the conversation contained happy news for a change. Melissa felt that the reunion, and introduction of Michael and me into their lives, was like a final gift from Eric himself.

So, you might be reading this and wondering what prompted Lucy to pick-up the phone and call Catholic Charities after thirty-one years, just shortly after I contacted them. Well, that is what makes this story extraordinary.

Among Lucy's eight siblings is her younger sister, Annie. As a devoted and practicing Catholic, Annie believes that God sometimes speaks to her in the form of a dream. This might sound a little far-fetched to some, but Lucy believes Annie's understandings of these dreams, and Annie is comfortable sharing them with Lucy.

In April of 2009, on Holy Saturday of Easter weekend, Annie telephoned Lucy and said, "Our Lord has a gift for you." Lucy, without hesitation, was very accepting. She was excited about what it could be, and excited that God was paying such intimately close attention to her! Lucy then asked her what it was and Annie said, "You're going to meet your twins."

Easter Sunday, Lucy felt the urge to call Catholic Charities. At first it seemed like a crazy idea, and she banished the thought. After a day had passed, she realized it actually made perfect sense to call the office. She first tried to get in touch with Eric, and by calling the place where he worked discovered that he had passed away. That's when she called Catholic Charities and told Roslyn that she had reason to believe her twins might try to get in touch with her.

After the phone-call to Roslyn, Lucy couldn't help her preoccupation with meeting her twins, to the extent that she spotted a young man who looked to be in his early thirties and had features like Eric. She wondered for a moment if he could be her son. And, she actually asked him how old he was! It turned out he was twenty-something, so she promptly realized how crazy that was. She then decided to put the preoccupation of meeting her twins out of her mind but still trusted our Lord's message.

Eight weeks later on Trinity Sunday, Lucy and the family had gathered at Annie's house to pray the rosary. It was at this time when Roslyn finally called Lucy back and got her permission to pass along her contact information to me.

I feel truly blessed and humbly grateful that our search for our biological family turned out the way it did. Both Michael and I know that not everyone on a search of this nature meets the same outcome. We were blessed to have three moms who all loved us in a unique way that we can hardly fathom. We also would never have expected that a year later, in August of 2010, tragedy would strike and we would lose our mom. It was no doubt difficult for my brothers and me, suddenly being without the strong and loving woman who raised us. At the same time, though, after the healing began, I was in awe of how everything had come full circle: Judy and Lucy got to meet each other, and I believe our Lord sped-up the process so that their meeting would be possible. One thing is for certain, the Lord works in mysterious ways! Though we miss our mom dearly, it's a blessing to still have Martha and Lucy very much in our lives. And for that, we are truly thankful.

Brian Weldon

I Love You

I was raised Catholic and come from a big family. As the youngest of twelve children, I have plenty of nieces and nephews and lots of cousins, aunts, and uncles. All my life I had my family around me, so when my husband's job took us fifteen hundred miles away from my two oldest children and grandson, as well as all my other family members, I began to feel lonely.

My husband had never been very good at showing me affection. But when I was surrounded by my family I didn't realize it so much because they were giving me the affection I was used to. My husband's job was very stressful. He had taken on a job that had originally been handled by two managers and he received little support from his inexperienced boss. On top of it all, the company decided to launch a product improvement that wasn't completely proven. Having to deal with all of this, my husband was forced to remain at work for long hours each day. With all the pressure he was receiving from work, I couldn't add to it and tell him I was unhappy. I hadn't made any friends and my family was so far away that visits were hard to manage. Even more, I felt like a single-parent most of the time to our three teenagers.

We attended church, and my three children were very active with youth groups. My son and I even attended a church-sponsored retreat. It had very inspirational speakers who shared their own life stories. We broke out into small groups and discussed what we were looking for. I wasn't really sure what I was there for, and I didn't even know what was wrong with me. I told the group my issues with my husband and being so far from home. They were very caring and said they would pray for me. At the end of the retreat we had the option to have others put their hands on us in prayer. I wasn't sure at first and just sat and watched not knowing what to ask for. I began to notice the people coming back to their seats seemed more at peace so then I went up to a couple, and they began to pray over me. That made me feel good and I sat back down.

I sat alone and as I prayed, I heard a voice say "I love you". Of course my eyes popped open, but when I looked around no one was near me. I was very nervous and wondered who said that and why. So I closed my eyes again and began to pray. Again I heard a voice say "I love you". Once again I opened my eyes; no one was near me.

I thought, *was that in my head or was that someone close by coming up beside me and saying those words?* But I did not recognize the voice. So once again I closed my eyes and prayed, and once again I heard the voice say "I love you".

I began to cry from the warmth and peace that was washing over me. That was what I had needed all along, and I hadn't even known it until that moment. I needed to know I was loved. I had been so preoccupied with feeling unloved while being away from my large family that I had forgotten that the Lord's love is the only love I need.

Lisa Bruce

An Opportunity Created by God

It was August of 2007. Saint Margaret of Scotland parish's church was under construction, and I felt called to offer up my artistic abilities. I have always been fascinated by Byzantine icon painting. *Perhaps I could try to recreate one of these paintings for the new church. It would be a vertical set of paintings: a triptych (a three-panel type of medieval, religious art) with Jesus in the middle and either angels or apostles to the sides.* I was thinking big—at least four feet high by two feet wide each.

I was ready to approach Father John, the pastor of the church, with my idea; however, I was unsure of the reaction I would receive from him. He knew me, but not well. I wasn't a consistent churchgoer by any means. My children were young, and going to church usually turned out to be a disaster for my family and those sitting around us. I tended to use that as my justification for why I often didn't attend Mass. However, I'd just committed myself to going to church every Sunday because this was the year that my oldest would be making his First Holy Communion. I didn't want to lead a family that only showed up on Christmas and Easter; I wanted to set the right example for my children.

It's amazing how you can do something when you simply say to yourself, "There is no option. You are going to attend church on Sundays." I didn't know it at the time, but God was setting me on a great path that would lead me on a journey to a more fulfilling relationship with Him. That year was truly a turning point in my spiritual life, with both my return to the Church and with what I consider a sort of reconversion, thanks to the journey I now recount.

I asked Father if there would be a wall that could accommodate the picture I imagined. Possibly a hallway or somewhere off to the side. Instead, Father said, "Come with me. I think I have just the spot for you." We went to his office, and he pulled out blueprints. According to Father, there was a certain wall that the architect himself said "...would scream for a large piece of art."

Father couldn't have been more right—the wall he referred to would be situated above the "gathering space," or foyer, of the church. A painting in this location would be the first thing people noticed as they entered. It astonished me that he offered such an opportunity. As an artist, I had only shown Father one of my pieces. It was rather brave of him. I didn't feel worthy.

I told Father that I was extremely honored, but that I would have to rethink the actual piece of art. The wall was more horizontal than vertical, so my idea of a triptych wasn't going to work. I set off to do research and ended up in eleventh century Florence with an image of a famous mosaic "Christ in Majesty"; that is, the risen Christ with his arms outstretched in welcome. I decided to add a Scottish flair for the church's patron saint by creating a Celtic knot as a border.

I set to work that January in the boiler room of the newly opened church. The piece of art was to be eight feet by four feet, so construction needed to be done on site to accommodate the size of the piece. I wanted it to look like an ancient fresco from Italy or Greece that had been chipped off of a wall. My brother, who dabbles in carpentry, helped to build the frame that held the ten pounds of grout used to simulate plaster.

This piece of art was one giant experiment. I didn't know if grout would adhere to the rough side of the particle board; I didn't know how I was going to make the piece look old; I didn't know how the authentic milk paint I chose was going to behave. I began every day with a prayer that when I opened the boiler room door the labor I put forth the day before stayed intact overnight.

One afternoon, as I was approaching the end of the project, I applied a preparation that I thought was going to give me a crackle effect, and I left for the day. When I opened the door the next day, I found a cloudy thick film over the entire painting. One step forward, two steps back. But I didn't cry or panic, which would probably be my usual reaction to such a disaster. I repainted the entire Celtic knot (the most tedious part, of course), and I sanded and repainted parts of Christ and his robes.

Father would visit almost every day that he was in the building. Other people visited as well: the parishioners who took care of the floral arrangements, the artist who created the stained-glass art for the church windows, visiting priests, choir members, and curious passers-by. I felt that

I was able to share more than the final product; the visitors watched the creative process unfold. They asked lots of questions, some of which I couldn't answer. No one could picture what the end product was supposed to look like, because it looked like such a wreck sometimes on its way to completion. Heck, I'm not sure that I myself could picture how it would turn out.

Finally, the painting was ready for unveiling. The installation was scheduled for the Wednesday before Easter of 2008, and it seemed more than fitting—and even perhaps a bit coincidental—that the congregation would first see it during the solemn days just before the holiest day of the year. That evening confessions were being heard in the church, and at least four extra priests occupied the building. Father had helped me gather some interested parties for the hanging; he also arranged the use of an electric lift. We started at 6 p.m. … and after a few failed attempts at determining the best way to hang this one-hundred-fifty-pound behemoth, the painting was on the wall.

It was ten at night, and we were all cranky, tired, and hungry from our long, frustrating evening. But we were grateful and happy, I most of all, to see Christ welcoming us into the new Saint Margaret of Scotland Roman Catholic Church. The confessions wrapped up, and all of the priests came out into the foyer to check out the new addition. It was then that I asked Father, "What was it that made you entrust this project to me in the first place? After all, you hardly knew of my work. God knows what sort of monstrosity I could have created." He answered that he just somehow knew it would all work out. It's like we both just knew that there was a greater force involved. I can't think that the church just *happened* to need a piece of art for that wall, and that I just *happened* to step forward to offer.

For me, that painting is my chef d'oeuvre, my life's masterpiece, and I know that I'll most likely never do another piece like it. Tears come to my eyes as I write this story, just thinking of how God gave me such an amazing opportunity. He was there, leading me by the hand through the entire process from conception to completion, and certainly through those times when I doubted that my vision would ever take form. My creation did take form, and the final product differed greatly from what I had in mind. But what resulted was more wonderful than I could have ever imagined—thanks to Him. And when I see that painting every Sunday, I know that there is no way I could have done it alone.

Julia Hulings

"Christ in Majesty" created by Julia Hulings, 2008

The Small Miracle at the University of Delaware

"[...] Jesus said, 'Let the children come to me, and do not prevent them; for the kingdom of heaven belongs to such as these.'" (Matthew 19:14 New American Bible (Revised Edition) [NABRE])

Hearing these words from our Lord led me to search for ways to respond to His call to bring the little children to Him. *But how*, I thought. Our Lord answers this question simply through scripture:

> ... [a scholar of the law] tested him by asking, "Teacher, which commandment in the law is the greatest?" He said to him, "You shall love the Lord, your God, with all your heart, with all your soul, and with all your mind. This is the greatest and the first commandment." (Matthew 22:35-38 NABRE)

What better way to love our Lord with our whole heart, our whole mind, and whole soul than to receive Him, visit our Lord more frequently, and bring our children with us—to spend quality time with Him either at Mass or at His Church where He dwells in every tabernacle throughout the world? There is a tabernacle in every Catholic Church; the word *tabernacle* is derived from the Hebrew *mishkan*, meaning residence or dwelling place. It is located near a continually lit red candle, signifying our Lord's presence. There is no more beautiful expression of love in our world than to spend time with our Lord, especially at the Holy Sacrifice of the Mass—the non-violent martyrdom where Jesus, The Lamb of God, is always celebrated... an act that He commanded through love.

I was raised to attend Mass every Sunday and Holy day. No matter where in the world I was, whether on a family trip, at a friend's home, or even if I had to walk to Mass in the middle of a snow storm, I was expected to be at church every Sunday. I knew I always wanted my children to experience the same commitment. I wanted to honor our Lord's request to bring our children to Him at His celebration, especially on the Sabbath, the day that He commanded us to rest and worship.

As most parents with young children can attest, just getting your children to church on time, let alone trying to have them sit still, not argue, and be quiet is quite a feat in itself. But on one occasion during Mass in northern Virginia, I was kind of proud of my son's outbreak in the silence, when normally I would cringe with embarrassment. Father was giving his homily on the Saints—our Brothers and Sisters in Christ acknowledged for their holy and virtuous lives who are now believed to be our helpers in Heaven—and what it meant to try to live like how our heavenly role models did while on earth. Then he rhetorically asked our congregation, "Who can be a saint?" At the top of his little lungs, my son yelled, "Liam can!" All of the people, including Father, laughed. *That's right*, I thought, *we can all become saints, but how can I help my children to strive for heavenly sanctification? Surely I could do more. Perhaps I could take them to visit our Lord more frequently at the holy tabernacle, but where?* Our family was in the process of moving to Delaware, so we didn't have a new church home yet, but I knew where to find Him: any Catholic Church.

Once we arrived in Delaware, I searched for an open church—and by open I mean unlocked, where my wife and I could bring our family to pray before our Lord in the holy tabernacle. Even just spending five minutes in front of the tabernacle, no matter what your faith, will bring you a peace and joy like you have never experienced. All are welcome, everyone:

> Some scribes who were Pharisees saw that he was eating with sinners and tax collectors and said to his disciples, "Why does he eat with tax collectors and sinners?" Jesus heard this and said to them [that], "Those who are well do not need a physician, but the sick do. I did not come to call the righteous but sinners." (Mark 2:16-17 NABRE)

After all, are we not all sinners? Our Lord reminds us of this in Romans 3:23: "all have sinned and are deprived of the glory of God" (NABRE). Remember when you go to the tabernacle, you go to our Lord who says,

"Come to me, all you who labor and are burdened, and I will give you rest" (Matthew 11:28 NABRE). Each time I saw a Catholic Church and could, I stopped my car to try to spend a few minutes with our Lord to receive His healing power of rest! However, most churches I encountered were locked—an unfortunate sign of the times and increased security posture that we live in now. But, low and behold, I found one that was almost always open at the University of Delaware's St. Thomas More Oratory.

Each day and into the night, the Oratory is staffed to accommodate the spiritual needs of the university students. On almost every Tuesday evening throughout the year, something very special happens and still does: the most Blessed Sacrament of our Holy Lord, Jesus is exposed allowing all an opportunity to adore Him. All are welcome, giving our community the opportunity to participate in a beautiful tribute to our Lord Jesus in His humblest form. The Dominican Priests, lovingly and tenderly, pay tribute to Jesus through prayer, music, silent meditation, reflection and an opportunity to receive the Sacrament of Reconciliation. This sacrament is a wonderful opportunity and call to conversion, a confession of our sins and celebration of forgiveness instituted by Christ, who delegated this authority to men (our priests):

> "But that you may know that the Son of Man has authority on earth to forgive sins"—he then said to the paralytic, "Rise, pick up your stretcher, and go home." He rose and went home. When the crowds saw this they were struck with awe and glorified God who had given such authority to human beings. (Matthew 9:6-8 NABRE)

The ability to partake in the Sacrament of Reconciliation is a truly freeing occasion of God's unconditional mercy calling us all to forgive one another. Christ our Lord knew He would not be with us always, so He sent us his shepherds, his priests, the "Fishers of Men" (Matthew 4:19). Jesus said, "[…] 'Peace be with you. As the Father has sent me, so I send you.' And when he had said this, he breathed on them and said to them, 'Receive the holy Spirit. Whose sins you forgive are forgiven them, and whose sins you retain are retained'" (John 20:21–23 NABRE). Christ can heal all sins, but in His infinite wisdom he knew we needed the counsel of a priest to hear these words. If you have not been to confession in a long time I urge you to free yourself of your burdens and release the chains of sin through this powerful gift. If you have never been and are reading these words, I pray that you will take the steps to come home to Christ's Holy Catholic Church.

Tuesday nights at the Oratory's Eucharistic Adoration is an occasion for all to adore our Lord in His most exposed and humblest form and partake in an opportunity for silent fellowship with other families trying to do the same. In my case, this time of adoration was an opportunity for a group of men to meet as fathers who desire to lead our families on the narrow gate. Our Lord says in Matthew 7:13-14, "'Enter through the narrow gate; for the gate is wide and the road broad that leads to destruction, and those who enter through it are many. How narrow the gate and constricted the road that leads to life. And those who find it are few'" (NABRE). Don't all of us desire to find it? Perhaps spending more time with Him is one way to answer His call to the greatest commandment: to grow to love our Lord more. Most importantly, it is an opportunity and occurrence for peace and grace for our hearts that we all need so that one day, God willing, we can all make it to Heaven. Knowing this, I have longed to share the experience of kneeling before the humble presence of the Lord with my children as much as possible.

On some Tuesdays at the simple Oratory my wife and four young children would come to visit with our Lord in this relatively quiet environment. Well, quiet until we arrived. During these special evenings my children have had the opportunity to kneel before our Lord, bringing with them their small prayers and intentions. On one occasion, during intentions, my daughter Elizabeth, who was just six years-of-age at the time, asked for prayers for the people of Japan in the aftermath of the earthquake, tsunami, and floods that wreaked havoc on so many. I was overwhelmed with joy to hear my daughter so maturely and unprompted offer up a prayer of petition for those in need. But as you can imagine, my children would eventually grow restless and want to explore the inside of the Oratory, look at the pictures of the holy cards, and ask if they could have another glow-in-the-dark rosary. My other daughter, Isabella, would often draw pictures of our Lord Jesus on the Newcomers Welcome Card located behind each seat. She would proudly present them to the young priest and say, "Look Father, look what I made for you," as I turned red in the face and sheepishly apologized for yet another card not used for its intended purpose. More often than not, my children would whisper loudly to each other saying, "Shhh! don't talk," as the other one responded, "No you SHHH and don't talk!" "No, you shhhh!" "No you, no you…Dad, the other kids are talking!" … Needless to say, at times it was like herding cats and asking mooing cows to be quiet.

Embarrassed by the noise in front of the other parishioners, I tried to endure the innocent disturbances because I could not help but keep hearing the words of our Lord in my mind, "Let the children come to me…let the children come to me." Those words kept echoing through my mind over and over. After all, how can I let the children come to Jesus if I don't bring them to Him? *I must bring them to the Exposition of the Blessed Sacrament whenever possible,* I thought, for this is a rare occasion where one can worship under his true presence which He Himself instituted:

> "I am the living bread that came down from heaven; whoever eats this bread will live forever; and the bread that I will give is my flesh for the life of the world." […] Jesus said to them, "Amen, amen, I say to you, unless you eat the flesh of the Son of Man and drink his blood, you do not have life within you." (John 6:51-53 NABRE)

Knowing that this humble piece of bread is the source of all life for us on Earth, I cringed with embarrassment when my children misbehaved, but I kept repeating, *Here I am Lord. You said,* "Let the children come to me," *and I am bringing them to you and I know that they sometimes misbehave and yes, perhaps, I could do a little better at teaching them self-discipline and sitting still, and perhaps that is why You said those words.* Our Lord knew it was that kind of behavior—innocent or unbridled—that prevents us parents from wanting to endure such situations. Despite those innocent disturbances, our Lord asked that we bring our children to Him.

Learning the hard way that an hour of adoration may be just too much for them, on a few occasions I brought them in for just ten minutes at a time. Surely, just ten minutes has to be edifying to their souls, especially souls not yet stained with the effects of serious sin. On one Tuesday evening my three-year-old, Sofia, asked me to take her to Adoration. "Sure," I said, for how could I possibly deny this request of bringing my child to Him?

That night, as we entered our Lord's home at the Oratory, there stood the striking monstrance with our Lord humbly exposed in the form of bread. How abundantly He must love us to humble Himself to the simplest form of all staples, unleavened bread, and how perceptive of our Lord to link the creation story from Genesis (14: 17-20) of the use of bread and wine in a ritualistic celebration, where Abram is blessed by the king and Priest Melchizedek, as we are blessed today by Christ with his body and blood in these two same mediums. Once you begin to understand the link and realize the significance of the experience of transubstantiation, you can't help but be filled with emotion as you stand, kneel, sit or prostrate yourself in front of our Lord, like we are able to do at Eucharistic Adoration. The only other act in this world that is actually greater is to eat and drink of His body and blood.

This second most important act of our life, and on this particular Tuesday night of Adoration, was like no other that I had experienced before. There was only one other woman present in the church, quietly sitting towards the front, so, my daughter and I took our place in the middle of the Oratory. Sofia quietly sat down next to me and then quickly hopped off the chair, as I thought, *here we go again, my little squirmy wormy can't sit still*. But this time, it was different. She asked to go up in the front of the monstrance to be closer to our Lord. I watched as she walked up to the monstrance, then stopped, looked over to her right, bent down, picked up a small kneeling stool and then placed it right in front and below Jesus, in the Blessed Sacrament. She then sat down and raised her outstretched little arms as if she were to be lifted by our Lord himself. Then a simple conversation took place during which she spoke, was silent, spoke, then still more silence, and spoke again. I watched in utter amazement and looked at the other woman to see if she was seeing what was happening before us. Her head was raised from prayer to witness this dialogue. Then my small child got up and came back and took her place next to me. I asked her who she was talking to. She said, "Jesus." I said, "What did he say?" "He loves me," she responded. "Wow," I remarked, and then said, "What did he look like?" She stood up and smugly smiled as she perched her little arms at her waist and said, "He has brown eyes, like me."

There is no doubt in my mind that my little daughter saw our Lord that day, not just in His simple bread-like form, but in His bodily form. I will cherish the memory of this small miracle for the rest of my life. For remember, "[…] Jesus said, 'Let the children come to me, and do not prevent them; for the kingdom of heaven belongs to such as these'" (Matthew 19:14 NABRE). We are trying, Lord; we are trying, like so many others, to bring our children to you and we remember all are invited to his table of plenty. Won't you go and spend just five minutes with Him?

A Prayer by the Mother of Fr. Idongesit Etim, Associate Pastor at Saint John the Beloved

Lord out of Your love, You gave me my children. They do not belong to me, but to You. So I give them back to You. You know that I am imperfect and plagued by faults; please let them turn out as You will, a perfect offering from You and lead them back to Heaven, where they belong, to forever dwell in Your presence. Amen.

W. F. S.

A Testament of Faith

My name is Janet Alexander, and I give a witness of what Jesus has done in my life. As a child I attended a Catholic school where I was taught by the Franciscan nuns who were instrumental in my religious education. The nuns wore black habits with large white bibs and a silver and black cross that hung in front of their bibs. A brown rosary hung down the right side of their habit while a white cord was worn on the opposite side. The white cord had three knots, each representing one of their vows: poverty, chastity, and obedience. During recess when I was in the fifth and sixth grades, I remember kissing Sister's cross and thinking, "You must have to be a good little girl to receive a cross like this." It was not an expensive cross—something today that would only cost about five dollars—but it was beautiful to me.

Time passed and I grew up; I married and had a daughter. After sixteen years of marriage, my husband and I divorced for unreconcilable differences. I left the church for approximately ten years. During this time, I was filled with unhappiness, guilt, and loneliness. I went to confession three times because I knew God was calling me back, but the priest couldn't give me absolution because I needed an annulment.

I eventually remarried a non-Catholic and was married by a Methodist minister in his home. I still couldn't find forgiveness in my heart for my ex-husband. I started to pray to the Blessed Mother to keep me, to have God forgive me, and to help me. I eventually found myself going back to church on Saturday evenings at the 5:00pm mass. I wanted to receive the Blessed Sacrament so badly; there was such a yearning in my heart.

After going to Mass for a year, I felt like I needed to do more for the Church. So, I volunteered every Tuesday at the Delaware Hospital for the Chronically Ill to push the wheelchairs of patients to Mass. I gave myself this penance to make-up for the masses I had missed over the past ten years. I also committed to praying the rosary every day to help me in my healing.

I finally reached the point in my heart where I felt the need to apply for an annulment and convinced my husband, who I'm married to now, to also apply because he needed one too. We had to wait a year for the approval of the annulments. It seemed to take forever, but in the end I was so happy when they were approved. On December 17, 1988, we were married in the Catholic Church. What a joyous occasion!

In January of 1989, I felt a calling to serve as a lector at Mass. I was surprised by this calling because I had never read in front of anyone in my life; I was very shy. I spoke with the parish priest, and he said if I wanted to be a lector then he would talk to the coordinator about placing me on the next schedule, which was made every three months. So I practiced from that day on to be ready to read in church when my time arrived.

On the first Sunday that I was scheduled to read, I was very nervous. Knowing it was my first time ever doing something like this, I asked God for His help in reading that day. While driving to church I prayed, "Dear Lord, this is the first time I'm reading in Your church. Please let me touch someone's heart, especially someone who has been away from church like I have, and let them know how merciful You are."

When I arrived at the church, I went into the building and didn't talk to anyone—I was too nervous. I went directly over to the book of the gospel and took it to the back of the church. At the time, the lector carried the gospel to the altar; today the deacons do it. While carrying the gospel in my hands, I began to hear a sound come over both of my ears. It was a swishing sound that encompassed my whole being. I didn't know what it was; I had never heard that sound before, but later I realized it was the wind of the Holy Spirit. When I reached the ambo, an elevated pulpit, to place the book of the gospel readings, a voice said to me, "Janet, something is happening to you." At that moment I completely disappeared on the altar: I heard nothing; I saw nothing. Then, this wonderful peace came over me; the Holy Spirit read for me.

After I experienced this awe-inspiring sensation, I took my seat for Mass where I remained. When I was finished with the reading, I returned no longer afraid. As the reading had just proclaimed, I became an ambassador for Christ. The gospel reading for that Sunday was about the prodigal son who returned to his father. Oh, how our Lord rejoiced because I was the prodigal daughter! Through the acceptance of serving as a lector and the participation in the sacrament of confession, I had become a new creation. I once was dead in sin, but now I am alive in Christ and He rejoiced in my return.

When I walked from the ambo to return to my seat, my vision was glowing—beautifully glowing. People came up after Mass to tell me how they felt when I was reading. They were filled with an excitement upon hearing me read God's words. I told them the Holy Spirit was with me during the readings. Since then, I haven't been afraid to read at Mass.

Around this time, I had joined the parish Sodality Group. About two weeks following the first Sunday I read at Mass the group was preparing for a bake sale. In doing my part for the group, I was busily making Italian pizzelle cookies alone in the kitchen of the church when a lady came in and approached me. She told me she had heard me read at church a couple of weeks ago and that I was the reason she was here tonight to go to confession. I turned to her and realized I did not know her, so I became interested in what she had to say. She told me her name was Lorraine and went on to say, "You touched my heart. I have been away from confession a few years. I didn't know how merciful God was until I heard you read." Well, I began to cry because I thought back to the prayer I had said in the car on the way to read at Mass. She had no idea what I had just experienced; she was a stranger to me. She probably thought I lost my mind. I gave her a great big hug, and she told me that she was so happy to be here but she was very nervous because she had been away from confession for so long. We were both blessed with God's real presence at that moment. Since then we have become good friends.

As time went on, I became the parish environment and art coordinator, taking care of the flowers on the altar and sewing the banners. I continued with this work for eight-and-a-half-years. In addition, I joined a group of ladies to make cord rosaries for the missions while Sodality provided the funds for the materials. We sent (and continue to send) the rosaries all over the world, to Africa, the Church of the Holy Sepulcher in Jerusalem, all the missions in India and the Philippines, the prison ministries, all the local school children, the local hospitals, and to wherever there was (or is) a need.

One Sunday a visiting priest said Mass for our parish. He asked if there was a Eucharistic Minister present to help with communion. No one stood up. So then he asked if there was anyone who wanted to be a Eucharistic Minister. So help me, I did not think myself worthy of such an honor, but my hand went up. When it was time, Father called me forward and I went to the altar to help with communion. After this, I was asked to take a class to become a Eucharistic Minister. Little did I know that when I signed up for the class, Lorraine had done so too. We were the first women to become Eucharistic Ministers at our church.

Lorraine and I started to take communion every week to the homebound, as well as to the hospital for the chronically ill. I continued with this work for at least twenty years until my knees gave out. I had to have both of them replaced and could no longer walk the long halls of the hospital. I did, however, continue to visit the homebound with the Eucharist. Through the mercy of God, I met a wonderful friend, Marietta. She became homebound after receiving open-heart surgery at the age of eighty-five. I would visit her weekly over the course of two years to bring her the Eucharist. She would always have a cup of coffee with me on those days.

One morning in particular, while we were visiting, she brought a cloth out to the table. In the cloth were two five-inch crucifixes: one was gold and black, and the other was silver and black. Marietta proceeded to tell me that these belonged to a Josephite priest, and she wanted me to have one of them. She gave me the silver and black one, the same kind the Franciscan nuns wore that I used to kiss at recess when in school. I thanked Marietta for such a wonderful gift and told her that I would cherish it forever. This brought a smile to my face and filled me with wonderful joy. I believe God gave me my own cross to have and to hold. Finally, I had become a "good little girl". God never forgets the goodness in your life.

Around that time, I was praying the rosary and realized that God wanted me to lead a renew group at church. While meditating upon the third glorious mystery, The Descent of the Holy Spirit upon the Apostles, I felt God's love. Now, I'm seventy-eight-years-old and I've been married, so I've had marital love and I've had family love. But this is a love that went deeper into my soul. It went to my hands and to my feet and to my head; to my hands and my feet and my head; to my hands and my feet and my head. It was the most magnificent feeling of love that I have ever had in my entire life. I believe it was the love of the Holy Spirit who dwells within our souls. He knows us when we're up, when we're down, when we're sleeping.

He can fill us in an instant with the knowledge that sometimes takes a lifetime to learn. And, He can do it readily.

In response to this calling, I talked with the parish priest about my interest in leading a renew group but told him that I did not have the education or the experience to become a teacher. I felt that maybe since our Lord helped me to feel His love, then He would help me learn to teach the Renew Group. Well, the group was formed and it consisted of about nine or ten of us ladies. In preparation, we attended different seminars to learn how to conduct meetings for small groups of people. Through our work in the Renew Group—over a period of four years during Lent and Advent—we helped people with their family problems, their setbacks, and even helped some people find their way back to the sacraments and to the Church. This was a wonderful experience.

At another point in time, I was on the altar reading at the weekend Mass when I saw a beautiful white light. I thought it was the sun at first, and then I looked more closely at the light and saw that it was moving, almost with diamond clarity like it was alive. Looking to the right of the church, the people appeared a colorless gray. Looking to the left, I saw the very same thing except for where the light was shining. The beautiful white light shone over one man and a child. I felt our Lord's presence of peace come over me. I kept looking as best I could, while continuing to read the Word of God at Mass. The light was absolutely beautiful compared to the surrounding colors. I couldn't explain it.

After Mass had ended, the gentleman, over whom I witnessed the light shining, came up to me in the hall. He introduced himself and said I knew his daughter. He wanted me to know that while I was reading he saw a light shining over me. He had never seen anything like it before. I assured him that it must have been the Holy Spirit that he saw because I felt His presence when I read.

When I went to Mass the next morning, the words of one of the readings included "the light of Christ" and "sanctifying grace". The hair on the back of my neck and on my arms began to rise. I knew the Holy Spirit was telling me that this was what I had witnessed in church with the light. Because I had gone to confession the day before and was without sin and completely filled with grace, just like the man in the pew and the little five-year-old boy, I believe God blessed us with His loving gift of sanctifying grace. I praised God and thanked Him for showing me this wonder.

Through my years of ministry, I have found that a relationship with God will grow through prayer, love for one another, and attending Eucharistic Adoration, which is where a person meets with the real presence of Jesus through the exposed consecrated Host. Our parish chapel, St. Ann's, held Adoration every Tuesday morning from 9:00am to 10:00am, which I attended for four years until I moved to a different church. This special hour filled me with love, joy, and peace because Jesus really is present in body, blood, soul, and divinity at every moment when you give yourself to Jesus in Adoration. He will lead you into a new life; much strength and consolation to overcome all our trials in life can be received during this time. We are like grains of sand on this earth and Jesus calls each and every one of us to personally come and be with him in Adoration; He is there for *you*. It is a special time to quiet your soul. You will find the peace you are searching for as well as more love and patience for your family. If you find time for God, He will put everything in your life in order.

In November of 2012, a young lady at my new church asked me if I could read at morning Mass for her because she and her family would be moving to the beach for the summer. I jumped at this opportunity. So every Tuesday morning at 8:00am, I would read the epistles and the Intercessory Prayers for the Sick if the deacon wasn't at Mass to do the readings. A month had passed when this same woman who I had been reading for had asked me to take over her Adoration time, 9:00am to 10:00am on Tuesdays. I told her that I was ready when she needed me. After being asked, I was sitting in the pew during Mass and listening to the readings someone else was doing when I heard a voice say to me in my ear, "Don't you recognize the time?" For the life of me I questioned, *now what does that mean*? Then, it came to me all of a sudden: our Lord had arranged the opportunity for me to have this specific Adoration time, 9:00am to 10:00am—it was the exact same time I had when I attended St. Ann's chapel at another church. I had nothing to do with making these arrangements, which is what the voice meant. How great a feeling I had for this to happen! I told the monsignor about this great happening in my life and he said that God must have missed me during the six months I was away from Adoration. He knows that I do love Him!

Over the past twenty-eight years of ministries I have come to find that there are several important factors in leading a good, strong, faith-filled life. For example, if you are married, then you have chosen your vocation as a family. When you have children, you become their teacher. As parents, we are responsible for seeing that our children get the proper education about Christ and His church. In praying, we bring great peace to ourselves and to our children. If you put God as the head of your house, then you will be surprised at how secure your love becomes.

Furthermore, by following closely the Ten Commandments and teaching your children to do the same, you will be following in God's will because there before you is what God wants you to do. I'm not saying everything will be easy because it won't—that's how life is on Earth. But, you will see that the more you do for God, the more you will want to do. And, He will give you the grace to do all you want to do in His name. Someone asked me not too long ago, "Don't you think you do too much?" My dear people, we can never do too much for God. He knows how to slow us down if we need rest.

We are called to have charity in our hearts and show God's love wherever we go. Try to find time with the rosary; it's a string of beads that serves as our reminder about the life of Jesus on this earth. The mysteries of the rosaries reflect the stories of the Bible. Pray to our dear Blessed Mother, Our Lady of the Rosary, that she will take you to her son. For when I was a lost soul, she led me to Jesus and helped me to attain the peace I was looking for and needed. With His divine mercy, He forgave me of all my sins. I have found peace, and he offers this to everyone. Remember it's our own choice. He offers us eternal life or eternal death. So my dear friends in Christ, have great desires for good in your heart and Mary will present them to Jesus. Saying over and over again the "Our Father", the "Hail Mary", we are saying, "I love you". You will receive wonderful graces if you persevere in prayer.

Praying the rosary will call abundant divine mercy for your soul and you will do good works. If you practice saying it daily in a family group, it will help create harmony in the family. It will bring greater peace; "The family that prays together stays together." Some families find it difficult to find the time to pray together because of busy schedules, as do individuals who find it difficult to set aside time for prayer, but I want to help you understand that saying the rosary is not a labor that will overburden you. It's not a complicated task like algebra. It is a gift of grace that will change your life, lift you up, and give your life vitality. Through the rosary you will begin the journey of the life, death, and resurrection of Jesus and you will follow Mary's life as the mother of Christ.

I remember hearing about a mother who prayed a rosary every day for her son. He was on drugs and ended up in the "gutter". In the end, the only person that would help him was his mother. When he went back to her she said, "You just say one 'Hail Mary' every day if you're going to stay here." So he did. And little by little he was blessed with grace from God. He thought in his soul, *God is calling me to be a priest, I don't believe it*. He did become a priest and he traveled all over the world sharing his story. The incredible road to his vocation began by praying a simple "Hail Mary".

When we pray, we make acts of virtue of faith, hope, and love. When we pray we are lifting our soul to God to adore, to thank, to praise, to ask pardon for ourselves and for others, to make known our needs to God. Prayer expresses our complete dependence on God and our reliance on Him for all that is good in our life. Prayer seeks neither to persuade God to do something He is unwilling to do, nor dissuade Him from doing something He intends. Genuine prayer changes us, not God.

God is our Father, and he wants to give you the gifts that you ask for. Praise Him and thank Him at the same time as if you have already received your request. All you have to do is invite Him into your heart, your life. He will only come if you invite Him. Do trust in God who made you and everything you see around you; all things are possible with God. He loves you dearly.

In your life support your church whenever you can, however you can. I promise you God will give you a high return on your investment; He loves us very much. All you have to do is truly love Him in return. None of us have lived a sinless life, and through the mercy of God we can be made holy by His loving grace and by asking for the forgiveness of our sins through reconciliation. In the Sacrament of Reconciliation Jesus is there between you and the priest. He already knows your sins before you admit them, so ask for His help in remembering sins: the big ones, the little ones, recent or long ago. We need His mercy and He wants to give you unconditional love for the rest of your earthly life. God wishes us all to be saved and has given us the choice of eternal life. He wants us to share in His eternal happiness in heaven. He is very much aware of all your crosses in your life, and He wants to help *you*, but God is waiting for you to invite Him into your life and into your family's life. He is always a gentleman because He will patiently wait for your invitation to enter your heart. He will not force Himself where He is not wanted because He gifted us with free will. If you invite Him into your heart, He will lead you to the truths in all things.

If you knew a remedy or a medicine that would bring peace to the world and quiet all your fears, wouldn't you want to know what it is? The ultimate remedy is the Holy Eucharist— the body, soul, and divinity of our Lord Jesus Christ—and to keep ourselves united with Christ, we pray to Him, my dear friends. Prayer will give graces in abundance during our lifetime and peace at our death. Jesus is the way for peace in your soul. He will give you His peace.

Janet M. Alexander

A Funny Thing Happened on the Way to the Table Last Sunday...

It had been a while since our extended family had been together, and a lazy afternoon cookout seemed like the best opportunity to see everyone and catch up on their lives. Since my mother died a few years ago, getting everyone together for the holidays had proved to be more complicated with every passing year. She was the matriarch of our family and made sure that no matter how busy our lives became, we could always count on breaking bread at her home with regularity. We always had a tradition at Thanksgiving of joining hands before the meal and singing the doxology for our prayer. With the passing of Mom, we started doing it whenever we were all together at home for a meal.

It was raining that day and all plans for volleyball and outdoor activities had to be abandoned. As everyone began to arrive we were left scrambling for ways to entertain my four young nieces and nephews. Soon our house was filled with twenty-five hungry people laughing and carrying on as I raced around organizing the contributions to the meal and preparing to call everyone to come and get it. Because it was such a casual affair, I decided that no one would want to sing and pray, and I would dispense with our tradition. After all, it wasn't a holiday or even a formal meal, just dogs and burgers, and find-a-seat-anywhere-you-can type of gathering.

After checking that everyone knew the food was ready, I walked into the dining room to find them all standing around holding hands, spilling into the living room and waiting for me so they could sing the doxology. As I looked around at the faces of my family sharing the ritual that connects us from our past to present and into the future, it sounded like the angels were singing and God was smiling.

A. B. Douglas

Unidos y juntos

I stepped off the cramped plane, my legs protesting at the movement. As I headed up the ramp and into the Philadelphia Airport, I couldn't believe I'd been in Mexico only a few hours ago and that a life-changing adventure in another country had finally come to a close.

The last time I had been in this airport, I'd been a frightened college sophomore off to my first study abroad trip. I'd never been gone from home for so long on my own, but for an entire month I was in Mérida, Mexico to learn Spanish. I hardly knew anyone on the trip, and I knew I was about to fly straight out of my cozy comfort zone and into the unknown. Little did I know about the great friends I would make or how my faith would grow.

Within the first few days of living in Mexico, I discovered how vulnerable it feels to be an outsider and to barely speak the native language. I had studied Spanish for five years, but the classroom had been somewhat formulaic with its predictable topics and scenarios. Out in the real world, I had to think on my feet… and I wasn't quite ready for that. I stumbled over simple phrases, forgot easy words, and often ended up doing a lot of miming and hand-waving to communicate. But again and again, I was struck by how patient people were with me and how they encouraged me in learning their language.

My Spanish improved as the trip continued, but I was by no means fluent and certainly couldn't understand everything people said to me. Despite that, one of the things I really wanted to do while I was studying in Mexico was to attend a Catholic Mass and see how Christians worshiped in another country and another language. I came from a Protestant background, and I knew little of the Catholic faith, whether it was in Mexico or America. However, I'd learned about the large presence of Catholicism in Mexico. Participating in a Mass would be another part of my cultural exploration here—and turn out to be another big step in my walk of faith.

Near the very end of my trip, I got an opportunity to go to a Mass with my friend's host family. It wasn't what I expected at all. I'd pictured an ornate building with lots of colorful decoration and stained glass. Instead, the open, airy sanctuary was almost plain. It made it easier to focus on the Mass itself, which was important for me as I quickly got confused on what I was supposed to be doing. There was no bulletin or program; the members seemed to know things by heart or simply follow the instructions given by the priest. My Spanish still being somewhat limited, I scrambled to stand up, sit down, and bow my head with the congregation. I mouthed words to songs; I didn't have the benefit of a hymnal or even a screen with song words, like we had in the contemporary services back home.

I was so busy trying to keep up with everything that when the time for Communion came, I wasn't really ready. Maybe I never could have been.

Everyone reached for each other's hands and linked them together. We began singing a song in Spanish, which I can't say I properly sang with or even remember. But I felt something in that sanctuary as we lifted our voices and stood together. I felt not like an outsider, but instead a part of something familiar and powerful. The Holy Spirit moved through that room that day. It bound us together, not in a common language, but in a common faith that speaks without words, straight into our hearts and souls. I felt at peace, and I felt at home.

This moment has stuck with me for years and has made me a stronger Christian. In the past, I don't think I had recognized the true meaning and power of Holy Communion. I'd let it be a ritual where I went through the motions but didn't stop and think deep enough about the meaning behind it. That day in Mexico, though, I pushed my understanding of Communion a little further. It is a remembrance of the New Covenant, of the sacrifice Jesus made. But I don't know if I'd ever realized before that it is also a memory we build on every time we eat the bread and drink the wine. That it is a moment in which barriers drop away, languages and borders don't matter, and we share in one common truth—Christ died for us all to free us, and we're one family.

Once, I'd walked down a ramp into a foreign country and felt small, lost, and confused. I didn't know I'd be leaving a month later with the feeling that I was leaving behind a new home and family. Now, sometimes when I take Communion in my home church here in the USA, I close my eyes and picture that sanctuary I visited in Mexico. I know, somewhere out there, are more children of God sharing in the same meal. Across borders, we're still linked together in faith: *los hijos de Dios, unidos y juntos*—the children of God, united together.

Morgan Prettyman

*Acknowledgements:
Thanks to Li Zhao for her help checking my Spanish grammar.

Learning from J.C. ...

One morning in 2006, I was awakened by my son's alarm clock. Since he seemingly had no intention of shutting it off, I went into his room to wake him up, only to find that he was dead. I was completely devastated: my son had lost his life at the age of twenty-seven.

Three or four days after my son passed away, I visited my church to make arrangements for the funeral. I shared with the pastor that I cried day and night; I was inconsolable. I told him that I was trying to make sense of *what* had happened and *why* it did, a person so young with no visible illness or anything dying suddenly. It was something completely horrible that happened.

Father said that God would be there to help me through this difficult time. Well, I must have been inspired by the Holy Spirit during our conversation because after that, I went into the church and turned to the image of the Virgin Mary, and I said, "Holy Mother, please give me the strength that you had when your son died, so that I am able to cope with the passing of my son." From that point onward, I prayed to Mary for her intercession on my behalf.

I still cried day and night, at all hours. While I was driving, I would often pull over to the side of the road to dry my eyes because I couldn't see through the blinding tears. Then, to my surprise, on the first anniversary of my son's death, I stopped crying. It was as if someone had turned a switch in my head to, "No more tears."

With the tears no longer clouding the vision of my heart, I began reflecting on the precious memory of my son. I often thought to myself that he looked like an angel; he was different. My son had a genuine heart. For example, when I used to complain about others to my son, he would ask me, "Why do you always see the bad things in people? Why don't you see the good?" I would simply reply, "Well, people drive me nuts!" He would simply answer, "Mom, you have to learn to be more patient and understanding with people. Try to put into practice what you hear from God when you go to church and pray." It was through his example of compassionate respect for others that I was able to see how he viewed everything around him. He was a pure soul!

I remember a particular time when I was having issues with my neighbor because he would park his car directly in front of my parking space. My immediate reaction was to fight with him because his actions made me so angry. Aware of how I would respond to the issue, my son would say, "Let me handle this for you." He always took care of everyone while striving to maintain the peace.

Throughout the course of my son's life, we would have discussions about the Bible, and he would always have questions. Since I often did not know the answers to his questions, I would tell him that he would have to ask God when he got to heaven. After he had passed, I thought to myself, *now he knows the answers to all of his questions because he's there to ask God.*

After my son had died, I told my sister, "I am going to start practicing everything that he used to do, and maybe I can become a better person. I will just follow in his steps." And, I did: I became a better person. I still have a long way to go, but I have changed a lot since that tragic day.

To help me along my path to healing, I joined a bereavement group within my church. During our meetings, I have told the members that I believe we, parents of deceased children, are chosen by God for this particular path because He knows that by our faith and our strength we can handle something so terrible. There is nothing more terrible than losing your baby, your child, but Jesus had said that we will be given only what we can handle.

Through this tragedy, my faith has grown tremendously, and I often find myself thinking about the Virgin Mary and the loss of her son. This woman did not do anything to deserve such a tragic loss. And her son, the Son of God, did not do anything to deserve the horrific death he suffered. Mary witnessed a death that no other parent has ever had to witness happen to their own child.

This realization led me to think about what she had to endure as a mother. She had to stand in front of that horrible cross, seeing her child tortured while not being able to do anything to stop it. And then, after Jesus had died, she had to cope with the loss of her son before she was granted understanding from the Holy Spirit. Yet, through all of this she never wavered in her faith.

I thought if she had the strength and courage to endure the pain of losing a child, then I am going to hold onto her for strength to endure my own loss. It is only through faith that a person can keep going during such a devastating time. To get through the tough times, you have to learn how to look at the situation in a positive light, as difficult as it may seem.

I never thought I could be happy, but I have grown so much through this experience that today I am a happy person. My happiness comes from within by being so close to God and by knowing that Jesus is with us. He said, *I will be with you until the end of time.* And now, when people ask me, "How can you cope with the loss of your son?" I simply tell them, "By the grace of God."

I am the person that I am today because of this experience. It is only through the love of God that I was able to come out of this tragedy a much happier, love-filled person. I suffered first in order to find God, but sometimes a person has to be taken outside of the confines of their own perceptions of life in order to truly understand the power of God's love. It is amazing how God works into every part of our lives.

Ruth Peré

2

God is Strength

"The weakest part of my life can become the strongest part of my faith."

– Author unknown

Strength through Suffering

To compose a life within a few pages is a difficult task. When said life is your own, it seems an even harder task, especially when you have had a life filled with troubles and joys. I was born in the Dallas Fort Worth area on November of 1992. I am the middle child of three and, as my mother would put it, I am the glue that holds us together. Almost immediately following my birth, the doctors and nurses must have been concerned about something because they only allowed my mother to hold me for a few moments before they whisked me away. My parents assumed this was because I was born twenty-five days early. But, when my mother asked if I was alright, the nurses just dismissed her worries and assured her that everything was fine; I was just a little jaundice.

By my two-week checkup, the jaundice had cleared, but I had developed something on my scalp that looked like cradle cap, though it did not behave like it. My mother had also pointed out to the doctor the small bumps on my body that closely resembled "prickly heat", a form of heat rash. But, the doctors dismissed her concerns as nothing more than a needless worry from an over-reacting mother.

At about four-months-of-age, the doctors were examining my ears because I was having constant ear infections. I had just finished another round of antibiotics the day before when my doctor noticed that the infection appeared as if it had penetrated my ear drum. As they were examining me further, the doctor questioned a rash that my mother had believed to be just a normal diaper rash that did not seem to ever go away. Since it did not look like a normal diaper rash, the doctors advised us to see a dermatologist.

After meeting with the dermatologist a couple of different times it became very apparent to my mother that the doctor had no clue what the rash was either. Making a long story short, the dermatologist performed a skin biopsy. A few weeks later, the results were in and, as things would turn out, this so-called-rash ended up being so much more than they ever dreamed it would be. I had a rare blood disorder called Langerhans Cell Histiocytosis (Histio), which is considered to be an autoimmune disease. I was only five-and-a-half-months old when my parents were informed that this disease was known to be fatal among infants.

With this particular disorder, the body creates an overabundance of white blood cells called Histiocytes, which roam the body looking for anything foreign and harmful. It may seem that an excess of Histiocytes is a good thing, but once activated they can attack anything deemed foreign—even parts of the body that we know are essential for life. This means that bones, skin, eyes, vital organs, and even the brain can be at risk of an attack from Histiocytes. It is uncertain just what causes these cells to become active, but one belief is that a severe injury could spur it into action.

If this is the first time you have ever heard of Histio, I am not surprised. It only affects five in a million people who are born every year. When I was first diagnosed, it was two in a million. Every person who is diagnosed with Histio is unique in how the disease affects them and there is no set treatment protocol. Thankfully, the doctors know how to diagnose it better now than they did when I was first born. I hate the idea of people suffering and having no idea what is causing it.

Fortunately, the disease was only active on the surface of my skin at the time of my diagnosis. However, because it was only on the surface, my parents were warned that at any time it could go internal. They needed to remain watchful for the occurrence of any unexplained fever as this could mean that the Histio had moved internally.

Once I was diagnosed with Histio, the dermatologist could no longer treat me. Since there were not any specialists in the area who could treat me, we ended up having to go to Children's Medical in Dallas, Texas. Once there, I was treated with prednisone because my disease was only external and the rash cleared up. It was even believed that I never really had any ear infections, but rather it was the Histio that had become active in my ears.

It was not until I was about ten-months-old when strange things began to occur, one of which was the unexplained fever that my parents were warned to watch for. This fever was like nothing my parents had ever seen. One minute I would be burning up, then the next my temperature would drop drastically. On top of all this, I was drinking like a fish. I had stopped eating and all I would do is drink. The amount of fluid would be so plentiful that my stomach would feel ice cold and protrude right out. I would then proceed to vomit the liquid that I drank only to repeat the process all over again. But, every time my mom took me to see the doctors, I was not displaying any symptoms that she spoke of; I just sat there and smiled at them. This went on for five weeks until they noticed that I was not gaining any weight but actually losing it. Then, I was finally hospitalized to find out why this was happening.

So, at eleven-and-half-months of age I was admitted to the hospital where they began the testing. The doctors discovered that the disease was active on two of my vertebrae: at the base of my brain stem and in my pituitary gland causing Diabetes Insipidus (DI). DI is often confused with sugar diabetes, but in truth it has nothing in common with it. DI affects an entirely different part of the body. Sugar diabetes affects the pancreas, whereas DI affects the pituitary gland. Your pituitary gland secretes most of the hormones for your body, one of which tells your kidneys to retain body fluids. Because that part of my pituitary gland was not functioning correctly, it explains why whatever I drank went right through me. Regardless of the amount of liquid I consume, I will dehydrate much faster than the average person if I do not take my medication. In addition to the damage being caused within my vertebrae, a hole in my left cheekbone was found.

As a result of these findings, I had surgery to implant a central line under my left arm (a tool that doctors use so they do not have to find a vein every time to administer the medication) and I started chemotherapy. I was treated in this manner until I was a little over four-years-old. The doctors' main goal was to cease the progression and put the underlying disease into remission.

In the beginning, the original treatment for my DI changed a couple of times. The medication I used then was called DDAVP, but how my parents were to administer it to me varied. At first they had to blow it up into my nose in a very difficult manner. They would take the medicine out of a syringe and inject it into a rubber tube. Then they would insert one end of the tube into my nose and the other into their mouth and blow the medicine up into my nose. If they did not blow hard enough, it would just come out of my nose, and if they blew too hard the medicine would just go down into my stomach and not do any good at all. Could you imagine how hard it must have been to put a little tube into a baby's nose and blow just right? Somehow I do not think I laid very still during this. Needless to say, this type of technique didn't work too well.

After that, shots of DDAVP were injected into my stomach twice a day. I remember my mother telling me that when it came time for me to get my injection, I would run over to a chair, stand on top of it, and say to her, "I just want a little bit in my tummy." She would agree, and I would come over for my shot. Every day, twice a day, this same episode would occur.

As I got older, DDAVP was squirted up into my nose again for the third type of treatment. But now that I was older it was administered slightly differently. The medicine was still inserted into a syringe, but this time my parents would remove the needle and stick the end of the syringe up my nose. They would then squirt the medicine up my nose while I took a quick sniff simultaneously. With that method we had the same problem that we did in the beginning: if my breathing and their squirting were not in sync, the medicine would either come back out my nose or go down into my stomach. The biggest difference between my first and third treatments of DDAVP is that with the third form of treatment I was old enough to tell them if the medicine did not work right. It wasn't until I was in my teen years that they developed a pill form of the medication that would help control my DI. Now, I take pills and they are called Desmopressin. This treatment is much easier to manage and easier to transport. Over all of the methods for administering the medication, I prefer this more recent one.

Unlike the difficult process I encountered with DDAVP, I experienced very few complications with the chemo I was treated with when I was young. However, there was one time, my mother believes, that I was accidently given the wrong kind of chemo because I had a terrible reaction immediately following the treatment. All of the places of my body that should have been soft, such as my cheeks and stomach, became either firm or hardened. It must have been extremely painful because I was told that all I could do was just lie on the couch and cry. Though I could talk at this time, I just called my parents' names and wailed in pain. I do not believe I knew how to describe what I was feeling because I was only three-years-old. I even lost all of my hair. I had never had this side effect before while I was on that chemo and I never did again—thank goodness.

Only after I had lost all of my hair did people realize that there was something going on with me medically. Up until that point, I was seen by others as just an ordinary little girl who danced with her older sister in the center aisle of church while the music played during Mass. This perception of me likely stemmed from the fact that I remained a happy child because I knew God was taking care of me and that He would never give me anything that I could not handle without His assistance.

As soon as my Histio went dormant, my mother was approached by researchers at Children's Medical who were studying the long-term effects in patients who had used central lines for long periods of time. Since I had used one for approximately four years, I qualified for the test, during which the technicians videotaped the x-rayed effects of some dye that was injected into my central line. While I was being tested, they asked my mother if I had ever complained of chest pains and/or numbness in my hand. It turns out, at four-years-old, I had blood clots all throughout my left arm and into my chest. The doctors later told my mother that if I ever had to receive chemo again or needed a central line, that I may have to be put on blood thinners.

During the time that my Histio was dormant, I lived a relatively normal life. My family and I moved up to Delaware to be closer to family who lived in Western Pennsylvania. I made a few friends, learned how to ride a horse, and took dance lessons. I went to church and learned about Our Lord and Our Blessed Mother. They have gotten me through a terrible time in my life, and I am ever so thankful. They have become my closest friends and are always there when I need Them.

As I reached my teen years, the feeling of being different from the others around me caused me to retreat within myself. I preferred to sit alone in the corner with a book, music, or paper and colored pencils rather than hang around other kids my age. I slowly grew out of that phase as I matured, but I still dislike hanging around people my own age. Though I have a few friends who are close to my age, I find it much more comfortable to be around those who are at least ten or more years older than me. I am not quite sure why that is. But, Jesus was and is always there when I need a friend, even if it is just to give me a hug when I am feeling lonely. He always helps cheer me up when I am feeling down. He even helped me come to grips with my medical disorder.

When I was a baby and it was found that the Histio had damaged my pituitary system, my parents were informed that I may stop growing at any point in time. Around the age of eight I did just that. It was then that the doctors prescribed to me growth hormone shots, which were then injected into my stomach every night before I went to bed. I was only on these injections for about two years before these shots caused me to enter into puberty sooner than expected, causing my growth to slow down. Because of this, I was prescribed another injection called Lupron. This was meant to slow down puberty so I could continue to grow taller. However, this injection had to be administered by a nurse and in the worst place possible—my rear end. I received these injections once a month for about four years.

Years ago when my Histio was active at the base of my brain stem, it was found that I had white mass changes that had taken place in my brain. Back then, little was known about what it would later develop into or even what it meant other than the potential for neurological issues later in life. Then, in my early teen years, the doctors discovered that I had scoliosis, which is an abnormal curvature of the spine. Those who have scoliosis usually have two curves in their spine: one that curves to the side and the other that corrects their center-of-gravity back to normal. When I was first diagnosed with it, nothing was done because the curve was only minor and we were told that many people who have scoliosis are not even aware of it. Even so, I continued going to an orthopedist to monitor the curve. As God decreed, He chose me to have only one curve, which led to problems with my balance. As my curve worsened, my balance did too. This led my neurologist to believe that the balance problem had originated from my scoliosis. On the contrary, however, my orthopedist believed that my scoliosis had nothing to do with the issues of my balance. It was not until my balance became alarmingly worse that the neurologist advised back surgery.

The idea of undergoing back surgery scared me to death. I knew what it would entail because a family friend had just gone through this type of surgery a year or so before. The surgeons had cut her open in a corkscrew motion all around the truck of her body. They then proceeded to remove her lower rib bones, fuse them to her spine, and screw a metal rod into her spine to straighten it out. So, after I got home, I prayed and hoped that I did not need back surgery. Well, I learned that I need to be more specific in what I pray for because, you see, about two weeks later we received a call from a hematologist who said that I did not need surgery for my spine, but instead I needed chemotherapy. After twelve years, my Histio was active once again! I would require surgery, but not for my back. Instead, I would need surgery to insert a central line for chemo treatments. God has a pretty good sense of humor. He did answer my prayer because I did not need the back surgery that I feared. However, I missed the bigger picture. I should have prayed, "Please heal my balance problems so I will not need *any* surgery".

Anyway, as I lay on the gurney waiting to be wheeled into the operating room for the surgery to insert my central line, I was crying. I do not relish the idea of having people cut me open, and I was worried that something would go wrong. While I was being taken into the operation room, I felt an unbelievable sense of calm come over me, as if God was telling me that everything would be all right and He would guide the surgeon's hand. I awoke a few hours later only slightly sore and ready to go home. God had kept His promise as He always has.

After about six months of receiving chemo treatments, the doctors approached my parents to see if we wanted to continue with the treatments. They did not believe it was doing any good because my balance was still declining. My parents decided to seek additional help and advice from the Histiocytosis Association in New Jersey, who then referred my parents to a specialist in Baltimore, Maryland. As a result, we changed doctors and my course of treatment to intravenous *immunoglobulin* (IVIG), which is a type of plasma treatment as opposed to chemotherapy.

When we visited the new specialist in Baltimore, we were finally informed that I do not just have Histiocytosis, but rather a more advanced form called Neurodegenerative Central Nervous System Langerhans Cell Histiocytosis with Diabetes Insipidus. Did you catch that one word in there? *Neurodegenerative.* That means that I will slowly, yet steadily worsen. So even though I already use a cane and have a leg-brace to assist me while I walk, I will continue to get worse. At the young age of twenty-two, I already have a laundry-list of health issues and I may even get more, if it is in God's plan for me. But, I will bear all that He gives me in confidence because I have chosen to offer up to Him whatever I am called to suffer to help someone else in need.

In moving forward with my treatment, my mother and I travel to Baltimore about once a month so I can receive the IVIG infusion. It takes about four hours providing that I do not have a reaction. If I do, then I am there for an extra hour or more for observation. I usually take some Benadryl beforehand so I will sleep through most of the procedure, but lately it has become a bit difficult to do so because the nurses come in about every half-hour to take my blood pressure and temperature. After a year or so of receiving the IVIG treatment, an MRI scan revealed some questionable spots. As a follow-up, I received a PET scan, which further showed that my Histio had been previously active, but it had stopped. It was no longer active. They are unsure if it was the chemo that stopped it, the IVIG, or if it just stopped on its own.

Yet, somehow, I still continue to worsen. My doctors now believe that my own immune system is attacking my central nervous system and causing my state to worsen. One summer we decided to stop the IVIG treatment since we were not convinced it was helping me at all, but then my balance declined at a much faster rate. So, IVIG seems to slow down the progression somewhat.

I now have a wheelchair that I use when I go on long excursions because my walking has gotten to the point where I have to concentrate so much on it that I quickly become both mentally and physically exhausted. My legs are so incredibly stiff at times that they are difficult to move; I drag my feet regardless of whether I have my leg-brace on or not, and I do it more frequently when I am tired. This is dangerous for me because a fall could cause my Histio to spur-up and attack the part of my body that was wounded by the fall.

However difficult it may be, I know that everything that I have been through and continue to endure is not without purpose. God has a reason for *why* He has given me these "disabilities". I have always said that I would rather it be me that has to experience the suffering than someone else, even if I do not know that person. My mother told me that while I was being created by God I probably asked Him if I could have all of the inflictions of my family placed on me. That actually sounds like something I would say because I do not like to see anyone else in pain, whether it be physical or mental. The funny thing is I am the only one in my immediate family that has had any real health issues.

In high school I wrote an essay on Histiocytosis and learned a great deal more about the condition. The statistic that has left a lasting impression on me stated that fifty-percent of infants diagnosed with Histio die shortly afterwards. Wow! If that is not a sign of God's loving-care, I do not know what is. Not only am I still alive, but God has helped me climb mountains—literally! With His help, I have hiked the Watkins Glenn Gorge in New York. It is a two-mile uphill hike. I also hiked the Chimney Bluffs in New York by Lake Ontario—a mile-and-a-quarter hike in the woods with an overgrown path strewn with large fallen logs. I even went on two separate hikes with my family in New Hampshire to two different waterfalls: Diana's Bath and Glen Ellis Falls. No one in my family thought I could do it, but God assured me that I could.

My attitude has not and will not change. There are times when I am sure that God is walking by my side holding my hand and helping me get to my desired destination. As I stated earlier, I believe I am going through this current suffering to help other souls. Who knows, I may be helping *you*.

God has wonderful unique plans for every single one of His children and some of them involve suffering. Some forms of suffering are harder to bear then others, but they are no more important than those that are lighter. We are all called to serve in different ways to help one another make our journey home. I choose to believe that this is not my home and I look forward to the next. In the meantime, I will continue to endure everything that God has in store for me with joy and humility. I know that He will not let my suffering go in vain. He has a reason for why He has entrusted me with this suffering, and I will endure it gratefully and patiently until I can lay it down at His feet once I reach the finish line.

L. K. Bauer

The Bridge Between

Once upon a time, I was born and raised on an island. In fact, I grew up and matured on this island. This island was the only world I knew. It was here I learned everything that made me who I am. It was where I educated myself, found religion, accomplished all my work and goals, and played with the human race.

My life was an ordinary one similar to all the rest of the people on this island. I lived with my wife and son in a big house full of "stuff". I had two cars of Power and planned to buy a boat of Prestige. I learned I could make myself happy by going down to the store of Possessions and buying more. I also learned to go to a local restaurant named Self-Satisfaction and indulge in those pies of delight to feel real good.

My house was in a big neighborhood with people of all kinds. Old and young, fat and skinny, rich and poor, smart and dumb, religious and non-religious, happy and sad; they were all there. In fact, I didn't really know or want to know any of them, so I mostly observed and gossiped about them and kept my distance. Then, it shouldn't surprise you that most of the yards including mine had fences around them, some seen and unseen, and this suited me just fine.

There were many streets in my neighborhood which I liked and frequently traveled. One of my favorites was called Self-Centered Street. I really enjoyed walking on this one because it made me feel very safe. I always knew how to protect myself on this street and when I was there no one could hurt me. Another of my favorites was called Self-Righteous Street. This was the most beautiful place on the island. Everything on it was exactly how I expected and wanted it to be. I was skillful at manipulating other people to remove any tree that had a different point of view or carried the disease of disagreement. I think it was my favorite one. The final street of my liking was Selfish Street. For some reason, I got most of my attention on this one and I didn't have to give anything back. Many times people would wave and say, "Hi," but most of the time I was walking too fast to notice. Those people really didn't matter to me.

Most islanders believed I was a self-starting, productive and active individual. Their praises always made me feel good about myself for one of my achievements included climbing to the top of Mount Pride. Actually, it was quite easy for me since I learned how from others before me. Everyone on this island will try it before death. Coincidently, most make it. And, would you believe it, my favorite activity was swimming in the river of Self-Sufficiency. I did not need or want any help from anyone while swimming. Fortunately, I survived a near drowning caused by a leg cramp. I refused the help from a person trying to save me.

Then another day came. I was standing at the island's shoreline trying to figure out what happened to my son. My son, who I thought would live a good life just like me on this wonderful island, became addicted to drugs. To deal with this problem, I used every island resource available including medical, education, social services, and law enforcement. Furthermore, I preached, punished and restricted my son's activity in an attempt to stop him. Nothing worked. Overtime, I became ill with an internal sickness causing crazy reactions to his behavior. I became overwhelmed with fear that led to anger, resentment, shame, embarrassment, and constant anxiety. I became plagued by and distraught over the consuming power of the drug of his choice. In the insanity of his feeding frenzy for it, it mercilessly devoured his health, wealth, joy, love, and zeal for life. In its relentless and unquenchable appetite for human life, his very heart and soul became its meal. I fought a good fight as a father should, but it only laughed at and mocked my love for him. In the end, it beat me down to a living hell and exhausted my energy. Yes, its power fed on the lives of a father and son whom in the simplest terms loved one another. I truly thought I lost control over my life on this island for the first time. I asked myself, "How could this happen to a mature and responsible man like me?"

Suddenly, I heard and saw a man swimming toward the island. Upon reaching the shore I asked where he came from and he said despondently, "From over there." I looked and saw what appeared to be another island. I asked him why he came back here and he said, "My dad was responsible for my troubles." He continued to say, "My friend, there are many ways back to here, but only one way to there." Shortly thereafter, a woman canoed up to the shore. I presumed she too came from the other island and asked why she came back here. She said, "I cannot live with my now sober husband, he doesn't pay me any attention." Before leaving she said, "My friend, there are many ways back to this island, but only one way to that island."

It was evident these two people were now living in misery like me. I thought something was different about that other island and I needed to know why. I obtained binoculars and a bull-horn to investigate. Looking through the binoculars, I saw an island very similar to this island with parallel land features and circumstances of life. Likewise, the inhabitants witnessed and experienced the consequences of violating God's name, ignoring time of worship, children dishonoring mothers and fathers, murder, adultery, theft, lying, coveting, death, disease, pollution, poverty, and natural disasters. I clearly saw streets with the same names as my neighborhood. However, there was one small but significant difference about the inhabitants. The people acted as if a quality of peace and serenity existed within and among them. I perceived a supernatural harmony and order existed in their lives. Something hoped for glowed from within. Yet, how could this contentment exist when their circumstances of life did not differ from this island?

At this point, I was motivated to get over there! I wanted what they had and knew a remedy for my problem was not to be found on this island. I used the bull-horn and yelled to a man on the other island's shore, "How do you get there?" He yelled back, "You must take the bridge." I took the binoculars and frantically looked for a bridge. I did not see one. Again, I yelled, "What bridge?" Whereupon he said, "It's the only bridge and way to get here." That was enough for me; I needed to find that bridge or build one to get there.

I used all available island resources to find the bridge and failed. Therefore, I determined I would build one. Using my learned leadership abilities and money, I aggressively motivated and manipulated other people to start building a bridge. This effort also failed from insufficient funds, exhausted personnel, and destruction of the bridge during a storm. In desperation, I found a fellow islander who was known to be wise. As it turns out, this person at one time lived on the other island but returned years ago because she lost a loved one and still blamed herself. She told me to go back to the shore, get down on my knees, ask for help, and patiently wait. I returned to the shore with a heavy heart where I humbly asked to see that bridge. The instant I felt the sand on my knees, I found what had escaped me for so long. Seeing the bridge, I hurriedly crossed over the one-way-traffic bridge to the other island.

This story ends with me living on the other island with people in recovery and restoration where I found it helpful to listen to the experience, strength and hope of others with circumstances that were akin to mine. I came to realize that although I physically aged on the island I grew up on, I was lacking in spiritual and emotional maturity. I learned there are many false ways to peace and serenity, but there is only one way to be right with my God and live with His peace in me. I discovered that the people who stay and live on this other island are absolutely trusting in an unseen Almighty power and they act in faith, love and hope irrespective of their circumstances. With a willing open mind and a receiving heart for the grace of God, their confusion was transformed to clarity by truth; their fears and worries were transformed into faith. Ultimately, they came to love the unlovable by finding the true riches of life: to love and be loved. I learned everybody and everything that came into my life were blessings given to me from a gracious God. I now know my son is a precious gift to me. It is now evident my son was being shaped by God's hands to become the spiritual being of God's perfect will. I must turn my son over to Him and accept the Divine outcome. Foremost, I see I was trying to be God to my son. And in God's mercy and grace, I now see the burden no more.

When I take an honest look back into the depths of my heart, the simple truth of the matter is I loved myself and the "stuff" more than I loved God. And not to my surprise, the Almighty God allowed me to become entrenched in success, possessions, pleasure, approval, and the religion of this world. And in turn, my heart was increasingly shaped by pride, self-centeredness, greed, gluttony, and love for possessions. And then, in His wisdom and providence, my world where I wanted to control the rules of life stopped when I was denied one last prideful achievement of wanting my son to be just like me. This circumstance challenged me to face the reality of my powerlessness and to accept the existence of an unseen Sovereign God. After many heart searching inquiries of what God wanted me to do, it became evident He asked me to believe and love Him with all my mind, heart and soul and to love others as I love myself. By living in His truth, I own the freedom to love and be loved without the burden of any circumstance in the seen world. Finally, my understanding and practice of forgiveness and unconditional love was buried within the circumstance of my son's disease of addiction.

As I wake up each day on this new island, I humbly pray to God, the Lord of my life, for strength and courage to remain on the island where I can become a better person living in the truth. I now know all too well that only one bridge exists to this place, yet there are many ways back to where I once lived. The island I grew up on is called the Island of Lie and Illusion and the island where I live today is called Truth and Reality. The difficult-to-find bridge is called Surrender. I wish everyone Godspeed on the journey to their own hearts and the strength and courage to find the only bridge that will lead them to it.

D. W. Litt

My Husband, My Hero

This story is about the time my family faced the possibility that my oldest daughter, Ella, had a brain tumor. The story, however, is not about Ella; it is about the heroic statement my husband, Phil, made in the midst of my deepest fears... the fear of losing a child.

I strongly believe when God gifts us with our spouses, He meticulously designs this person for us because He knows the important roles that each spouse will play throughout the sacramental life of the marriage. I believe this because I have witnessed it in my own marriage: He built Phil with gifts, wisdom, and knowledge that were specifically to be shared and revealed to me when the time was right for me to receive them. This story is about the time my husband became my hero.

Broken as I was, in the hallway of our bedroom dry-heaving at the fear that Ella had a brain tumor, Phil held me in his arms and said heroically, "If God wants her back, you have to *give* her back." I remember looking straight into his eyes, speechless. He said, "God gave us Ella on earth, and we never know for how long we will have our children. Tara, we have dedicated our children through the rosary to the Blessed Virgin. Give her now to Mary, and ask her to hold Ella and, if needed, deliver Ella to Her Son." I cried in Phil's arms and was up all night lying next to Ella thinking about his words.

The next day I went to adoration and the typical gorgeous gold monstrance, a vessel used to display the consecrated Eucharist, was not there. Instead, a wooden statue of the Blessed Virgin holding the *Eucharist* in her arms greeted me. At that moment, it became apparent that Phil's words were not his but *His*. I knelt down immediately, and I said to Our Lady, "Ella is yours." Immediately my heart was warmed. I didn't know what the future held, but I knew the Blessed Virgin was holding us and that we would press on.

In the need of prayers, I reached out to family and friends begging them to pray the rosary for Ella. It was beautiful to see friends emailing me back asking how to pray the rosary. The next day we went to the children's hospital for an evaluation by a neurologist. She was not at all convinced that Ella had a brain tumor. When the neurologist received the results of the MRI, she called me and said, "Her brain is beautiful." She went on to say that the MRI showed such a small abnormality that even if Ella did have a tumor, it was so, so, so tiny as not be worry-some. Although Ella's brain did display the presence of seizures, the doctors couldn't really explain why. Apparently, as odd as it may seem, it is a good thing to *not* know the source of the seizures. Ella was consequently diagnosed with epilepsy, which is a much better diagnosis than "brain tumor".

After receiving the phone call that brought peace back into my heart, I couldn't stop thinking about the Blessed Virgin Mary monstrance in our chapel. I rushed to pick Ella up from school, and when she came out to the car I grabbed and hugged her saying, "The doctor called, she said your brain is beautiful!" Ella's words to me were, "I know Mommy, Jesus came to me last night and told me He healed my brain." I didn't even know what to say, but we went straight over to adoration and the Blessed Virgin Mary monstrance was gone and the gorgeous gold one was back.

Occasionally I see the Blessed Virgin Mary monstrance, and all I can think is that someone else needs to be held by the Blessed Mother. I hope that they too are able to find the comfort and peace that can be found through the power of faith. Without faith, I don't know how I would have had the strength to endure this trial. God gifted the wisdom behind my husband's words because He knew it was what I needed to hear to help me move forward in this time of fear. He blessed me with my husband, my hero.

T. C. F.

Stepping Stones of Faith

I have always been a dedicated Catholic: never missed Mass, tried always to put others first, and raised my children with the knowledge that faith is the most important aspect of life. I lived an ordinary life. I married a very good man who shared the same faith and family values as myself and was a stay-at-home mom for twenty-two years raising four daughters and a son. It wasn't until 2009 when my faith was challenged.

My faith-life had a very routine nature up until the time when my friend, Meg, who was dying of cancer, invited me to join her rosary group. She started this group to help others develop a stronger relationship with God. At this point I felt my faith was being challenged: *was I being the best Catholic I could be?* Being a part of this group along with witnessing Meg's example led me to develop a more intimate relationship with our Lord.

During Meg's sickness, my father-in-law was diagnosed with ALS (Lou Gehrig's Disease) at age eighty-one. He needed our constant care as we watched this disease take over his body in a short six months. Prayer and daily Mass became a very necessary source of strength for me during this time. I can truly say that this was the very first time I could really *feel* the Holy Spirit's presence.

Somehow, the sickness, suffering and death of my father-in-law gave me a spiritual strength. I felt like there was more I should be doing with my life. While walking in the park one morning, I remember asking Our Lord, "Whatever Your will is for me, please let me know". I have never asked this before. Interestingly, it wasn't long after that when I was asked by our deacon to take over the Welcoming Committee at church. I felt honored to do this; getting to know the new families and welcoming them to our community is still a joy for me. This, I believe, was the first stepping stone our Lord sent me in response to my humble request.

The next stepping stone came along when Meg asked if our group would go with her to Medjugorje in Bosnia-Herzegovina, where the Blessed Mother still appears to the visionaries. Initially, I thought there was no way I could travel that far, but Meg traveled there twice during her illness and wanted to share her experience with all of us. She even paid for most of us to go on the trip. How could I say no?

Following her death, a group of forty parishioners from our church, including her children and our Pastor, went to Medjugorje. We felt Meg's presence the entire time we were there. I returned with a great sense of peace and courage to be more open about my faith. This trip gave me, as well as others in the group, the confidence needed to express more freely with family and friends the importance of having a more intimate relationship with our Lord. I realized that both the death of my father-in-law and of Meg were gifts toward my spiritual growth.

A year later, my faith was challenged again. After meeting a Ugandan Priest, Fr. James, and hearing the stories he told about the life and sufferings of the people in Northern Uganda who had experienced a twenty-year-long civil war, I was left with a deep compassion for them. It was at this time I felt a great surge of energy to help. So when Fr. James attended our Monday night rosary group, which continued after Meg's death, and expressed the need of a nursery school in the village of Anaka, he returned to Uganda with donations to begin the project.

We stayed in touch after he returned to Uganda. A strong bond was formed between us, uniting him with my family. Though the donations received from the community were very generous, they were not enough to cover the cost of the school project. I started reaching out for ways to help fund this so-desperately-needed school. I informed Fr. James of a Catholic foundation that granted money to such projects as this. I guided him through the challenging process of completing the application with the use of his weak internet connection. But, when it was submitted in July 2012, I felt very confident that the request would be granted.

Unfortunately, in November 2012, Fr. James received a letter denying his request. We were both deeply saddened by this news, but with unfound strength, I told Fr. James that this could only mean that more people had to be involved. I told him, "All things happen for a reason," and then we placed our trust in the Lord. I then prayed daily for the strength, knowledge and the right people to be placed in my path so I could continue helping Fr. James with this project. All the while, I did not really know what the next steps would involve.

During this time, I began selling paper-beaded jewelry for a women's group that was struggling for the basic necessities of life in the village of Wipolo. A box of paper-beaded jewelry arrived at my door in September 2012, sent by Fr. James. There were so many pieces that I labored with the thought of where and how to sell them. I decided to share them with the women from my rosary group and soon people were asking for the jewelry. I humbly took them to a local gift store and was surprised that they offered to sell them. Many caring people bought the jewelry, which enabled this women's group to buy two grinding mills and even start a small business. With the proceeds collected from this business, they were able to open a dispensary in a nearby trading center. The many who bought, sold, volunteered, or helped spread the word of the Ruganga Lakica Women's Group not only helped them to bring in additional income to care for their individual families, but helped an entire community. The "Gulu Beads", as they were named, are still bringing awareness to the struggling that exists within our world. I knew the Holy Spirit was behind me through all of this, pushing me one step at a time.

During his visit, Fr. James informed us that in Uganda a project could begin, stop when the money ran out, and then continue again as funds were raised. So, in December 2012, I encouraged Fr. James to start the building project for the nursery school. I remember asking him, "When will the ground-breaking take place?" Following this conversation, I thought to myself, *what gave me the authority to say that?* I not only wanted Fr. James to begin the school, but I wanted the people who contributed to know that their generous donations were being rightly used. I also had a great desire to go to Uganda myself to visit Fr. James and the people he talked so passionately about. My husband and family couldn't understand why I wanted to go and thought that I was unreasonable with my intent to find a way there.

On January 20, 2013, one year from his initial visit, the ground-breaking for the school began. Several fundraising events were planned to raise money. Month by month, Fr. James sent me pictures as the project progressed and I watched as the school developed from just a dream into reality. It was during this time when Fr. James fell ill with a very bad case of malaria, causing him to be hospitalized. Again, my prayer was a source of strength for him and myself, and my desire to visit Uganda intensified.

I assured my husband that if I went to Uganda I would travel with a secure group to ensure my safety. Now, I just had to find a group. I looked into different organizations, but all efforts failed. Finally, I discovered through the Archdiocese of Gulu's website that a few Sisters of St. Joseph from the U.S. were living in Gulu, Uganda. I sent them an email, asking if they knew of a group who would be traveling to Uganda. On the day that Fr. James was released from the hospital, I received an email from the Sisters of St. Joseph in Missouri saying that two of their Sisters were traveling to Uganda in May and they would be very happy if I traveled with them. I couldn't believe it! I would be traveling with two American Catholic Sisters who had experience in traveling to Uganda. I believed this to be yet another stepping stone that was gifted by God. I thanked the dear Lord and made my travel arrangements.

In May 2013, I arrived in Entebbe Airport and was greeted at the gate by Fr. James. I couldn't believe it; I was in Africa! The words of our Lord, "Blessed are the poor," became real to me as I viewed this developing part of our world. We traveled for one week meeting the people in the villages, the family of Fr. James, the children whom my family was sponsoring for school, the hospitals, churches and chapels, and some highlights of the country, such as the Shrine of Two Martyrs of Paimol and, of course, the building of the nursery school. We even distributed to families the goats that were bought with the money raised by religious education students and celebrated Mass with the people of Paibona. I felt a great connection during Mass when we prayed, "for the people of our Universal Church". Though there was no actual church structure—people gathered under a tree to celebrate Mass—we shared the same faith. It was wonderful and I felt right at home. I never once felt scared during my stay in Uganda. I believe it was God's grace allowing me to enjoy the beauty of the people and their country.

After my return home, I could not look at life in the same way. It was like I was stuck between two worlds. The people in Northern Africa had so little, yet their love of the Lord was so evident. They praised and thanked God for the little they did have. There seemed to be not much that stood in the way between them and God, unlike us in the Western world. We have so many things or obligations that distance us from being close to

God. I knew I had to share this experience with my family, friends and community.

One year after the ground-breaking, in February 2014, St. Catherine of Siena Nursery School opened its doors. Fr. James was very dedicated to the development of the school and the people in the village of Anaka. Approximately sixty children attend, several of whom were sponsored by people from the U.S. The school and property are fenced in and gated, the playground equipment has been installed, a third classroom will soon be added, and the children are enjoying learning at their new school—all guided by the Holy Spirit.

I don't think I could count the number of people who have been instrumental in making the dreams of the people in Gulu, Uganda come true. Several fundraisers were organized to continue supporting the developing nursery school, a goat and chicken outreach project was started, and the selling of the Gulu Beads has continued. All of which have been stepping stones in helping care for the poor.

All of these experiences have allowed me to grow in the love of our Lord. The best gift we can receive or give is the gift of love. My efforts are empowered by the Holy Spirit who is Love. I have grown closer to our Lord and can truly say now that I feel His presence in my life even stronger than ever before. I also feel such joy from all the individuals who have joined me in this mission of "Loving our Neighbor".

Mary Gispert

HIS Will be Done

My faith journey started out just like a lot of my fellow Baby Boomers. I was born in 1961 to devout Catholic parents, and I made my way through the sacraments; but then I drifted away from the Church after leaving home. Soon enough, I met a man I wanted to marry, and suddenly my faith mattered again. He was divorced, however, so I went to visit the local parish priest to find out what was involved with requesting an annulment. The priest said, "Just leave the adulterer!" I left all right…I left the Catholic Church behind and married in the Lutheran Church because we were welcomed there.

After a few years I became pregnant, and, you guessed it, I found myself yearning to return to my Catholic roots and desperately wanting to raise my baby in the faith I left behind so long ago. In spite of the treatment I had received from that priest as I approached my first marriage, I had discovered that my place within the Christian community was as a Catholic. It was the faith I knew and understood. And I believed that I had a place in the Catholic Church and prayed that another leader in the Church would see my zeal to return. I sought the council of a wonderful young priest in a different parish where my husband and I were welcomed back and my baby was looked at as a new creation. My son was baptized, and I had returned to the comfort of parish life. I even joined the folk group!

But while most of the parts of my life were moving forward, my marriage was slowly falling apart. My husband and I went through counseling, but we could not repair the damage that had already been done. We eventually divorced, and I found myself confronting the same stigma of the Church that my ex-husband had been in—I was now a *divorced* Catholic. Now what do I do? That question, however, took a back seat to a more important question: *How am I supposed to be able to keep a job, raise my son, take care of the house, and pay the bills all by myself?* Then, I met Paul.

Paul, like me, was newly divorced, with two daughters, Becky and Katie. We fell head-over-heels for each other almost immediately! We had much in common, and we complemented each other. We both came from big families and had difficult ex-spouses. Paul was easy-going and I was structured and organized: he was able to help me to "relax", and I was able to help him stay on the right track when things were going astray. Our only issue was that Paul was disenfranchised from the Catholic Church after spending all twelve years in Catholic school. He was still a believer, but struggled with the Church leadership and what he felt was hypocrisy. As our relationship grew stronger, Paul understood my desire to be married in the Church, so we worked together to obtain annulments of our first marriages. Soon we were joyfully planning our wedding day. We took our vows with our children by our side on the altar. Paul was so moved he began to cry; and it took everything I had not to start crying with him. It was truly a blessed day in August of 1994!

Our married life as a blended family had its fair share of challenges. My son Anthony lived with us, and the two girls lived with their mother close by. We had many moments when one of the children was in conflict with the respective stepparent. Some of those moments lasted years and caused us all quite a bit of heartache. I struggled to understand why so many obstacles were placed in our paths as Paul and I worked so hard to keep things together. We continued to attend Mass, and I found myself praying for relief from the daily drama that seemed to engulf every moment of every day. Little did I know that I was soon to discover real drama.

It was the weekend of the fourth of July in 2003. At 1:00am I heard the smoke alarm go off and I thought someone had burned some popcorn or pizza. But, my son suddenly burst through my bedroom door yelling we all needed to get out because the house was on fire! All of us made it outside, including the dog, and we watched in horror as flames shot out of the second floor. The fire departments arrived in minutes, and soon the fire was out. The cause was accidental, but we lost the entire interior of the second floor of our home, as well as some siding and damage to the first floors from water damage. Immediately I threw myself into managing the construction and purchasing of all the replacement "stuff". Fortunately, this undertaking required my strong organizational skills and unrelenting pursuit of perfection. Schedules and deadlines had to be met; and not just by me, but by the contractors too. I had spreadsheets and lists, on top of lists of "things to do", on top of working full-time and trying to keep my family together during this nightmare. The rebuilding process took almost eight months, as did the replenishing of all of our clothes and furniture, etc. By February the house was done. I had spent months on "auto pilot", and just getting things done took every ounce of energy I had. I was nothing but an empty shell.

But, throughout this ordeal, God had sent a messenger to me; I just wasn't listening. Her name was Lorraine—a family friend who was very active in the Cursillo Movement.

She had actually asked me to attend a weekend in October, but I had said, "No". The fire continued to consume me, and I refused to let anything come between me and my accomplishments. Lorraine didn't give up, though, and when she invited me to the March weekend, I said, "Yes." At that point I had nothing to lose and everything to gain.

The Cursillo Movement focuses on showing Christian lay people how to become effective Christian leaders over the course of a three-day weekend. The major emphasis of the weekend is to ask participants to take what they have learned back into the world, on what they call the "fourth day". The method stresses personal spiritual development. After my weekend I was full of the Spirit, and found a new peace in my life. The empty moments were now full of meditation and prayer. The fire, well...I finally learned what God wanted me to gain from the experience. You see, I realized I was alive! I had forgotten how to truly live. I was no longer just physically alive, but spiritually alive. God was present at what seemed like my darkest moment—and I could now see His loving hand leading me through it. It was the "spark" that lit the fire in my heart and soul. I was definitely on my way to a new relationship with Him.

My true faith journey began in April, just three weeks after my Cursillo. I stood out in the hallway of Christiana Hospital talking with my husband Paul's cardiologist, and realizing that he was desperately close to death as he was receiving his Last Rites. I knew before we married that he had a serious heart condition. He had a pacemaker implanted at age twenty-nine, and was in the early stages of congestive heart failure. As his heart disease progressed, complications arose year after year. But this time he had a rare, life-threatening reaction to a medication that caused aplastic anemia (the destruction of his bone marrow). This wasn't supposed to be happening—he was only forty-six! Obviously God had another plan for us.

All I could do was pray. I knew I had to continue to pray that God's will be done; as everything else medically had already been done. So I prayed, as did many others, and Paul cleared the crisis the next day. It was nothing short of a miracle to us.

Paul's condition, however, worsened over the next four weeks and it was decided in mid-May that he should be transferred to the University of Pennsylvania for a possible heart transplant. Paul underwent emergency surgery to connect him to a machine that would do the work for his heart until an organ donor was found. We were told that the machine was not an indefinite answer. A donor was needed quickly, as Paul's heart was failing in spite of every medical advancement and medication being used to sustain his life.

The surgery revealed another complication—an aortic aneurysm. An aortic aneurysm is a weakness in the wall of the aorta. There is a risk of rupture, which can cause severe pain, internal hemorrhage, and if not treated immediately, death! This would make the transplant surgery even more complicated because the repair of the aorta had to be done first, and believe it or not, the cardiothoracic surgeon explained that it was a more delicate and difficult surgery than the actual transplant. The wait for the news of the transplant seemed like an eternity. I prayed for God to touch the minds, hands, and hearts of Paul's caretakers. I also learned, through many tears, to pray for a family to hear the call of God to donate a loved one's heart to a very sick man.

We were blessed that our families were there for us. My in-laws visited Paul almost every day. My sister and her husband were a big help too. They visited Paul weekly in the hospital, bringing him home-cooked food and goodies. He looked forward to their visits because my brother-in-law was one of just a few men in our lives who felt comfortable going to the hospital. They were also a big help around the house through taking care of some much needed repairs. I was forced to learn to ask for help and to graciously receive it. Co-workers brought dinner for us when I was home so Anthony and I could share a quiet meal together. They were kind enough to be sure to include a "goodie" for Anthony. Anthony helped out by cutting the two-and-a-half acres of grass as well as accompanying me to the grocery store. His growth and maturity during that time were not lost on me. As we went to Mass together every Sunday, I found him reaching for my hand as we prayed the "Our Father". The comfort in that touch was a source of strength and peace for me and only reinforced that bond between a mother and her son.

We also kept in touch with Paul's daughters—Becky, who lived in Colorado, and Katie, who was more local. The relationship between the girls and their dad was a bit distant. As young women, they were following their own paths. I knew that neither of them was ready to face the possibility that their father would be taken away from them. Fortunately, Katie was close by and able to come up for a visit. I had talked with Becky extensively about her Dad's condition, and we both knew that my ability to fly her out for a visit was going to be complicated. I was just glad she had a chance to talk with her dad by phone.

Then the news came that the hospital believed an organ donor was available! The five-week wait for the transplant felt like an eternity. Instantly, my thoughts turned to the family who must have lost a loved one and would be donating their organs. I was torn between happiness and sadness. But I knew that the act of the donation was guided by God's will, and I was happy for my husband's second chance at life.

Paul left me at 10:00pm on June 22, and the six-to-eight-hour surgery began. I said urgent prayers throughout the night for the donor and their family, while pacing the hospital floor. I was wide awake through the night, but I surrendered everything to His will—my confusion, my sorrow, and my fear. My faith and the presence of the Spirit were my comfort all through the night—and I believe that God also sent an angel to escort our donor to heaven that early morning, and sent the Spirit to comfort their loved ones.

As the sun began to rise, I was awed by its beauty and its symbolism on this special day…the day the nurses call "Happy Heart Day". The doctor came in and told us that Paul's surgery had gone well, and we could see him in a couple of hours. My in-laws broke down. They were relieved, and so was I. But I couldn't cry; not yet. I had to see him first. A few hours later, I went to Paul's room and watched his EKG monitor show a *normal* heart rhythm and blood pressure, and I saw his once grey and pale skin was now a beautiful shade of pink! It was then that I finally wept. I sobbed uncontrollably on the shoulders of one of our favorite nurses, Katie. She held me, and she comforted me by saying that he was a miracle. I knew that the heart of another generous soul was beating steadfastly inside my husband's chest, giving him new life.

Days, weeks and months passed with numerous setbacks, additional surgeries, and major complications. Paul was in and out of the hospital until October of 2004. Amongst the chaos, I received an email at my office from Becky.

Dear Paula,

Just wanted to let you know how much of a blessing reading your emails has been. It is such a wonderful thing to be reminded of your love for my father. Your dedication throughout the toughest situations is undoubtedly a main reason why he is still here. Thank you for knowing that my dad's health was a reality, and marrying him anyway.

Your love and dedication to him is an example I will use in my own life with my husband and with my children…I just wanted to let you know this, because the thankfulness I feel every day that Dad can be a part of my future, and my son's future is more than words can describe.

Love,
Becky

I began to cry silently at my desk. I knew that God had touched Becky's heart, and gave her those words to share with me. Those words gave me strength to go on and brought us all closer together. We've had some incredible blessings since then. Our grandson, Gabriel, was born and we have celebrated our seventeenth wedding anniversary. Yet, our struggles continue as Paul is now in end-stage kidney failure and on dialysis, as well as oxygen dependent. And those vows we took, "In good times and in bad, in sickness and in health" were tested then, and are still being *lived* as we make our way along this journey. We are lifted up by so many people every day. Our friends, our families, as well as my parish family have all opened their arms and hearts in support as yet another chapter in my life unfolds.

It is said that "Courage is fear that has said its prayers". Well, I guess I could be called courageous. And much to my surprise, it has been an adjective often used to describe me over the past eight years. Believe it or not, I never questioned the path our lives had taken. I just wondered where it was leading us. And the path that I was led down was the path I desperately needed to follow. I finally found new priorities. I discovered that life isn't something to be controlled or scheduled. And I found out the hard way that my all-consuming need to have life planned in advance was a big reason why I merely existed instead of *lived*. I found a way to wake-up knowing that every moment is precious. And it took this experience for me to learn to let "Jesus Take the Wheel". I've become a lot more flexible, less judgmental, and more forgiving. I have even grown into enjoying a surprise or two! Then, it dawned on me that my personal growth and serenity began when the Lord had called me to Cursillo. I was called just in time to be able to bear the cross of my husband's illness with dignity, grace, and full of hope. And through the struggle, I emerged like a butterfly from a cocoon: newly born.

Paula Marsilii

To Trust in His Love

It was a typical Wednesday afternoon, my mom was visiting to lend a hand and spend quality time with her grandson. While she kept my son occupied with story-time, I discreetly slipped away for a moment to take a pregnancy test in order to put my lingering suspicions to rest. As I waited the long-lasting three minutes for the results, I sincerely hoped that the test would be positive and the two pink lines would appear.

When the timer expired, I anxiously grabbed the test, held it up to the light, and found that there was only one line: negative. My heart sank to my stomach and I placed the test back on the bathroom counter. But, as I turned to walk away, something caught my eye. Was there a second line after all? I sat and stared, readjusting my eyes, trying to see the faintness that seemed to be present. Unsure of what I had seen, thinking maybe the test had been faulty, I reached for a second test. I hesitated to open the box, and instead decided to wait another day so hopefully the pregnancy hormone (hCG), if present, would have the opportunity to increase.

The following afternoon I took another pregnancy test. I was shocked to find that the second faint line appeared yet again, but this time it was a bit darker than the previous test. I asked my husband, Brad, for his opinion and he too saw a faint second line. Well, as you can imagine, I didn't feel comfortable with the vague answer the dollar store tests were providing, and I just had to be sure. I rushed out to the local drug store to buy a higher-sensitivity pregnancy test. I quickly made my way back home and ran up to the bathroom to give it one more try. The third test results were very clear: positive—I was pregnant!

Brad and I were filled with joy! The previous year we had been blessed with the birth of our first child, a beautiful, healthy baby boy, and now we were expecting our second! We felt truly blessed and amazed at how everything was beautifully unfolding for our family.

A week had passed, and Brad and I were starting to make early preparations for our expanding family: deciding when to share our news with family members, tossing around baby names, and daydreaming about our future as a family of four. It was during this time that I had a phone conversation with a cousin to whom I revealed my pregnancy. As we were wrapping up our conversation, I became aware of some discomfort manifesting on one side of my lower abdomen, but I ignored it until I was finished with the phone-call. After I hung up the phone, I went upstairs to the bathroom, where everything was about to change.

I inherently knew that something was wrong. I could not stand. I could barely move. I could hardly speak. What was happening to me? I was severely vomiting, and my abdomen hurt so badly that it felt as if my body was fighting against itself and I was losing in my own battle. The only thing I could do was pray: I fervently asked God to protect me, to safely get me through the intense pain.

Brad came running upstairs when he heard the horrible sounds that were emanating from our upstairs bathroom. By the time he found me, I could hardly comprehend what was happening; I just knew something bad was taking place. Then, the bleeding started. Scared, confused, and horribly sick, I somehow made it to the bed to seek relief from the cold bathroom floor. Unfortunately, there was little relief to experience.

I was unable to sleep; the pain was unbearable, I had a constant feeling of nausea and was shaking uncontrollably. I phoned the on-call doctor, despite the late hour. She advised me that my body was likely threatening a miscarriage, and that I may have to go to the emergency room. In the meantime, I was to take some Tylenol and track the bleeding. We did not have any Tylenol in the house so my loving husband got out of bed to search for a twenty-four-hour operating store that carried the medicine.

While Brad was gone, I began feeling an incredibly immense pain in my left shoulder. The pain was so intense that I could not lie on that side of my body. What was happening to me? Something was going terribly wrong. I just prayed that my son would not wake-up because I was physically unable to get to him. Finally, after about a half-hour or so, Brad returned with the Tylenol. I took the medicine and experienced some much appreciated relief. The pain was still present, but it was at least tolerable and enabled me to get some sleep.

The next morning the bleeding continued. I was immediately scheduled to receive blood-work. I was physically weak and emotionally confused as to what had transpired in such a short amount of time. As things were obviously headed in a not-so-good direction, my mom came to stay with us to help care for my son while Brad took off work to care for me. I was sick and helpless.

A couple of days later I was awaiting the results of my second bout of blood-work. My mom had left the previous day, and Brad had returned to work because I was starting to physically feel better and thought that I would be able to handle things on my own. Not long after Brad left for work, I was overcome by a strange feeling and directly went to the bathroom. It was at this time that I experienced one of the most traumatic events of my life: I passed my baby. An overwhelming sense of emptiness and loss overcame me, and I was inconsolable. I immediately called my husband because I knew I needed him to be with me and, more importantly, to be there for my son. At almost six-weeks pregnant, my precious baby had died.

Following the passing of my baby, I continued to have blood-work performed to track my hCG level to ensure its return to zero. The absence of the hormone would indicate that there was no pregnancy tissue remaining in my body, which would then provide us with the "okay" to try to get pregnant again. Since we deeply desired having more children, we were hopeful for a quick recovery.

Well, as luck would have it, my hCG level was not decreasing. In fact, it began increasing! The doctor was concerned with how things were unfolding, so an ultrasound was performed to determine if there was any remaining pregnancy tissue. The ultrasound revealed that there was absolutely nothing in my uterus, indicating that the tissue was located somewhere else, such as in one of my fallopian tubes. These results, coupled with my previous symptoms, led the doctor to believe that this miscarriage was the result of an ectopic pregnancy.

An ectopic pregnancy is a pregnancy that occurs within the body somewhere other than the uterus, resulting in the death of the baby. It can be life-threatening to the mother because the baby becomes implanted in an organ that is not suited for nurturing life. Therefore, as the baby grows the organ will ultimately burst, killing the baby, destroying the organ and, in extreme circumstances, killing the mother. Unfortunately, if you have an ectopic pregnancy you are at an increased risk of having future ones because the tissue within the fallopian tubes may have been damaged from the implantation of the previous ectopic pregnancy.

It was at the point when the fear of an ectopic pregnancy was introduced that I reached my lowest low and my emotional strength plummeted, which in turn adversely affected me physically. The anxiety of the situation took hold and I felt completely alone, confused, and desolate. I *knew* that God was with me, but I did not *feel* His presence.

It was difficult for many of those around me to provide the support I needed during this time because it is very hard to relate to what is being suffered unless you too have personally experienced a miscarriage, and in this case, an ectopic pregnancy. I was angry with how events were unfolding and was emotionally exhausted from the grief of losing my baby and the lack of information that the medical community was able to provide.

Furthermore, Brad and I were being slammed left and right with medical bills comprised of sums that made our stomachs turn and plagued our feeling of financial stability. We were in trouble, and we knew it. Not only had this experience placed an emotional and physical toll on us, we were now faced with a huge financial burden. It just seemed like we were getting hit with one hard blow right after another; where was the light at the end of the tunnel?

Despite these horrible feelings, I continued to pray to God asking for His help. In response to my prayers, I received an email from a family member consisting of a message that spoke volumes to my suffering and in turn initiated the healing process within my heart. A passage from the email read:

> *"Nothing makes you feel better but time, prayer, and looking at [your son]. Embrace all these feelings and know your heart will heal with time ... just ALLOW yourself to hurt ... your feelings and fears are real and full of purpose. It's times like these that we are reminded how precious and miraculous the gift of life actually is.*

We don't hurt unless we love and we don't fear unless we care. We all do it in different ways, and some do it HARDER than others. God made you the way you are for a reason. And He gave you Brad and your family knowing each smile, fear, and tear you'll have. He gave you Brad because of each emotion you would have, and He gave you your parents and siblings (even your wickedly crazy extended family) knowing each feeling you would feel. They all have something you'll need to PRESS ON. Let them show you what they've got, and let God give you what you need."

I was deeply touched by the words that were written and felt as if a huge weight had been lifted from my shoulders. I no longer felt trapped by my emotions because I now understood that I had a right to the feelings I was experiencing and that God was actively present in my life. This gift of wisdom gave me the strength that I needed to move forward.

Now that my eyes had been opened to the shower of love that God was pouring over me, I began to see all of the tremendous blessings He had given me in the midst of such heartache. God's most comforting form of presence was made through my husband, to whom He granted unfaltering strength to carry me when I could no longer stand. God graced my husband with countless wisdom to share with me when I was confused or lacked understanding, all the while showing unwavering compassion towards me through every step of my trial.

God blessed me with a beautiful son, who radiates happiness everywhere he goes. I have never seen a person, let alone a child, light-up a room like he does. He is truly a little piece of heaven that has been given to us on earth. I told my husband time and time again, "I don't know how I would have gotten through this if we didn't have our son."

God blessed me through my mom who was able to provide the physical support that I needed by selflessly helping out with my son when I was sick. He blessed me through my mother-in-law who through her nursing background was able to offer medically advised answers to some of the questions I had about what I was experiencing. He blessed me through all of my family members and friends who were praying for me and offering words of support during this difficult time.

God further blessed me through my parents who were graced by Him to continuously share with my siblings and me throughout our lives the wisdom and knowledge of His healing and powerful love, the importance of prayer, and the understanding that faith in God is the stronghold of life. This gift of enlightenment played a crucial role in my ability to cling to my faith during a trial such as this.

And, most amazingly, God answered my pleading prayers for help that frightful night. I later came to find that the symptoms I experienced were "text-book" for severe internal bleeding and a ruptured fallopian tube. I found this out when I asked my midwife some lingering questions I had about the ectopic miscarriage because I was unsettled with how the whole situation had been medically handled.

Through these questions, I relayed all of the symptoms that I had experienced the night I started miscarrying. She stopped me and said, "Don't tell me you had shoulder pain." I said, "Yes! It was so severe that I couldn't lie on one side of my body." She looked at me with wide-opened eyes and said, "You could have died." She went on to say, "At the *very* least, you should have been rushed to the O.R. [operating room] because those symptoms tell us that you had a ruptured tube and internal bleeding." I knew she was right. I also knew that the reason I was able to have that conversation with her right then and there was because God carried me safely through that horrible night.

Though I was finally on the path to emotional healing, moving beyond the physicality of this miscarriage was not yet possible. I was informed by my doctor that I needed to have a hysterosalpingogram (HSG or "dye-test"), which involves an x-ray taken of the fallopian tubes to determine if one or both of the tubes are blocked or damaged (remember, I had symptoms of a ruptured tube). The idea of this procedure terrified me because I was afraid it would turn my fear into reality: the fear of not being able to have more children.

Not willing to leave anything up for chance, Brad and I quickly informed our immediate and extended families of the matter and asked for their prayers and participation in a novena to St. Gerard Majella, the Patron Saint of Motherhood, seeking his intercession for the healing of my fallopian tubes. I was extremely touched when we received such supportive and loving responses from many family members, which enabled me to draw strength in anticipation for the impending procedure.

> *"I know in my heart that God is working in your life to make you strong for the future. Take time to read the Bible and underline the verses that are applicable to your circumstances. Recite these back to the Lord, and claim the promises that Jesus makes. You will then see the true power of our Lord Jesus Christ and His word. Then you can enjoy and rest in the peace that comes with it."*

> *"I'm sorry you and your family have literally been put to the test. [My brother] stated in his most recent blog 'Hope…the infusion of desire, trust, and 'love for God'.' My hope and prayer is that your love for God will bring about the desires of our hearts that everything is O.K. and we just place our trust in His will."*

> *"Know that you and Brad are in our thoughts and prayers and if there is anything I can do to help you just name it!"*

> *"We will join in the novena […] We always pray to St. Gerard at the end of our rosary for special intentions like this! I know you and Brad will be blessed in the best ways since you put your trust in God … because He always wants to give us only the BEST! Love you and hang in there!"*

> *"I am at a loss for what to say, but my thoughts and prayers have been, and are, with you! Having never been pregnant or suffered a miscarriage, I have absolutely no idea what you must be going through, and I can't even imagine […] I started the novena yesterday and will absolutely be praying it with*

*you as well as praying, in general, that everything is O.K.
and no surgery is needed!"*

The morning of my HSG test had arrived, and I awoke with a sense of complete peace with whatever the results of the test would reveal. At that moment I had total trust in God that He would take care of me. This was the first time I had felt at peace throughout this whole ordeal, and it was very comforting knowing that everything was truly going to be alright.

> *"He is not afraid of receiving bad news; his faith is strong,
> and he trusts in the Lord." (Psalm 112:7 GNT)*

It was 2:00pm and I was sitting in the waiting room of the radiology center at the hospital. I was nervous and excited at the same time. I was not nervous in a negative way; it was more of an excited nervousness that one may experience before giving a presentation in front of a big audience. You know that you have fully prepared for this moment, but the anticipation of the event still gives you butterflies in your stomach. I was also excited for the test because I looked forward to receiving the closure that I had been longing for over these past three long months.

When my name was called to go back, I got up and walked with the nurse to the examination room. As I was walking I thought about how in just a short while all of this would be over, and whatever the outcome may be, it would mean that I could move past this miscarriage once and for all. She led me into the room and told me that the nurse practitioner who would be performing the HSG would be with me shortly. After I changed into the hospital gown, I sat down and waited for the nurse practitioner.

A little while later a nurse walked in without introducing herself and started rustling about. Then she instructed me to move to the x-ray table. She did not seem like a very "gentle" person, which alarmed me considering the procedure was a rather "delicate" one. As I sat on the exam table, I silently prayed that God ease my anxiety. Just as I had finished saying the prayer, this particular nurse told me that the nurse practitioner who would be performing the procedure would be with me shortly. Phew! I once again felt calm and at ease.

Moments later, the nurse practitioner entered the room with an extremely confident, professional, and pleasant nature. This was exactly the kind of practitioner that I had hoped would perform the HSG. She explained everything that was going to occur and asked me a few questions. Then, she prepared for the procedure and the test began.

After the dye had been injected, the x-ray was taken revealing the status of my tubes: unblocked and normal! Praise God! Our prayers had been answered, and I was granted closure, all in a matter of moments. It was a wonderful feeling; my words cannot fully express the gratitude that is deserving of such a blessing! God is so loving and gracious that it is overwhelmingly amazing! I truly believe I was healed by our Lord through the intercession of St. Gerard Majella and all the prayers of family and friends.

My feelings toward the outcome of the procedure were so powerful that I am reminded of the passage about the woman who touched Jesus' cloak:

> A woman who had suffered from severe bleeding for twelve years came up behind Jesus and touched the edge of his cloak. She said to herself, "If only I touch his cloak, I will get well." Jesus turned around and saw her, and said, "Courage, my daughter! Your faith has made you well." At that very moment the woman became well. (Matthew 9:20-22 GNT)

Unsurprisingly, in the healthcare world precautions are always taken, and although my tubes were shown to be fine, there is still no medical way to explain away my ectopic pregnancy. But, some things are not meant to be explained or completely understood, which is why God has gifted us with faith: the trust that we place in God to take care of us in all circumstances. I truly believe God held His hand over me through this entire experience, like a loving father protecting his child from all harm.

To top it all off, in just three months following the results of the HSG, I became pregnant! Nine-plus months later, Brad and I welcomed into the world a second healthy, baby boy. God so loved us that He blessed our lives with yet another gift of His perfect creation. And, the most incredible part of it all is seeing the presence of God's love in the eyes of our children.

This journey of my heart was a beautiful gift of God's love that resulted in the fruitfully abundant blessings of increased faith, healing, and peace. I am beyond grateful for the trial I was given because I have since gained a greater understanding about placing trust in God. Though I had thought I had trusted in God prior to the miscarriage, I discovered through this trial the areas in my life where I lacked in His trust. This new-found trust in God enabled me to find the much needed comfort during the most trying times of my miscarriage and, in the end, brought me peace of mind, heart, and soul. And, as with any lesson worth learning, this new-found trust would strongly be tested.

One Saturday morning in March, Brad and I were sipping our coffee as we discussed the day ahead of us. He would be leaving shortly that morning to help our good friends move into their new house while I stayed at home with the kids. Since we only had one vehicle, I had planned to stick around the neighborhood for the afternoon so Brad could use the van.

After he left, I decided to take the kids out for a stroller-ride to a store that was in walking distance from our house; I had a few items that needed to be returned. Before we left, I quickly ran upstairs to take a couple of Tums to ease the slight indigestion I was feeling and then we headed out the door. With my two-year-old in the stroller and my four-year-old by my side, we were on our way.

When we arrived at our destination, we walked directly to customer service to make the returns. I had planned to stick around for a bit to browse, but as we were finishing-up at the counter, a strange pain was manifesting in the right side of my abdomen. I thought maybe I was starting to get sick or my indigestion wasn't sitting quite right. Whatever it was, I didn't feel comfortable staying in the store, so we headed out the door. By the time we got outside, the pain had intensified enough for me to feel the need to call Brad. He asked if he needed to come home and I told him that there was no need. However, two minutes after we hung up the phone, the pain had worsened so much that I could barely walk. I was trying to get home at a pace that was painstaking to watch, nonetheless walk, all the while struggling to push the stroller and corral my other child. My condition was clearly worsening so I called Brad back to tell him that he needed to get home as quickly as possible. As the kids and I continued to slowly make our way back home, my mind was racing about what could be causing this much pain while inhibiting my ability to move. I found myself convinced that I had appendicitis. It was the only explanation that seemed to make sense.

We finally made it home where I was relieved to find the couch after I embarrassingly crawled up the steps to the front porch and through the door. I was in so much pain that I called my doctor to relay my symptoms, which led her to believe that I had appendicitis. She told me to go directly to the E.R. and that she would notify them I was on the way.

Scared and alarmed with the situation, I asked my two children if we could pray as a family. They both said, "Yes," and so I started to pray aloud. Just as the first few words were coming out of my mouth, my oldest son stopped me and said, "No, mommy. I want to say the prayer." Completely caught off guard by his request, I quietly said, "O.K." He then prayed, "Jesus, please help my mommy feel better." Simple. Calm. Direct. His little voice had so much strength and confidence behind it that it was evident, at four-years-old, my son understood the power of prayer. Though in pain, a smile made its way across my face.

Once Brad arrived home, we all loaded up into the van and headed to the hospital. After I entered the E.R., the receiving nurse asked me, "On a scale from one to ten, with ten being the worst, how much pain are you experiencing?" As I uncomfortably and awkwardly held myself up by the counter, I stated, "Ten." She then directed me to the waiting room where she said I would be seen momentarily. And, right she was: they were ready for me.

The E.R. nurse escorted me back to one of the stations and began taking my vitals and asking the routine questions about how I was feeling as well as gathering any pertinent medical history. I told her that I had an ectopic pregnancy two years prior, which immediately led her to the next question: "Are you pregnant?" I looked at her quizzically and said,

"No, I don't think so." There was no way I could have been pregnant—everything in my cycle had indicated I was not. Nevertheless, she had me take a pregnancy test right then and there.

When the results of the test came back, she walked over to me and said, "Congratulations! You're pregnant!" Initially I was confused, then my heart sank. I knew at that very moment it was an ectopic pregnancy and *not* appendicitis: I was going to lose another precious baby. I burst into tears. Confused by my reaction, the nurse asked what was wrong and I said, "I can't believe I'm having another ectopic." She tried to reassure me, saying that we didn't know for sure that it was the pregnancy causing my symptoms, but my gut instinct told me that it was. As the realization of what was actually happening to me began to sink in, I immediately thought about the scripture verse, "He is not afraid of receiving bad news; his faith is strong, and he trusts in the Lord" (Psalm 112:7 GNT). I knew what I was about to experience would be very difficult since I had already suffered an ectopic pregnancy—an experience that tore me down to my very core. But, through the grace of God, He lifted me to a place of peace and strength through that experience. He didn't let me fall then, and I knew He wouldn't let me fall this time either. So with God's Word being spoken in my heart and the trust that He would carry me safely through this impending heartache, I realized that He had already prepared me for what lay ahead.

Shortly after learning I was pregnant, I was transferred to triage—the maternity emergency department—where they started running all sorts of tests. Ultrasounds and sonograms were taken, yet nothing could be seen in my uterus. *Here we go again*, I thought. "It's still so early on in the pregnancy, that's why we can't see anything," the doctor told me. Then, a nurse came to draw my blood and had it sent to the lab. When the results of my bloodwork came back, they revealed that the hCG level was so high that the baby should have been seen through the ultrasound. Consequently, I was ordered to have a more sensitive ultrasound performed, which revealed a lot of internal bleeding throughout my abdomen. Moments later, the surgeon was sitting at my bedside.

The surgeon told me that a fallopian tube had likely burst and I needed emergency surgery. Though I had already suspected this to be an ectopic pregnancy, I did not expect surgery since my first ectopic did not require it. I was shocked. My mind started racing and my courage was depleting because this was something different from what I had experienced before—maybe I wasn't as prepared as I thought I was. My anxiety of the situation began to take hold. I was terrified because I had never been "put under" and the idea of the anesthesia absolutely scared me. I was almost to the point of panic when I recalled God's promise:

> "But I will bless the person who puts his trust in me. He is like a tree growing near a stream and sending out roots to the water. It is not afraid when hot weather comes, because its leaves stay green; it has no worries when there is no rain; it keeps on bearing fruit." (Jeremiah 17:7-8 GNT)

He was reminding me to trust in Him. So, I decided at that moment in fear to place my trust in God, believing that He would carry me safely through the anesthesia and surgery. And you know what, He made His presence known to me while in the hospital through various circumstances that only I would understand to be His divine intervention—His Fatherly presence.

These moments of His presence are so precious to me, that I hold them privately in my heart. It was His way of giving me the support and comfort I needed to get through the fear and receive the help my body needed in order to heal. As a result, I was at complete peace in the moments right before receiving the anesthesia and the only memories I have before being placed "under" were pleasant ones. Though the surgery lasted much longer than the surgeons anticipated due to unforeseen complications, I was brought safely out of surgery. As it had turned out, I had an abdominal ectopic pregnancy: the baby had attached to my liver. Enough said.

God took care of me every step of the way, just as He has promised to do for all who seek His help: "Do not be afraid—I am with you! I am your God—let nothing terrify you! I will make you strong and help you; I will protect you and save you" (Isaiah 41:10 GNT).

And, if you can further believe it, despite the odds that Brad and I were up against, God blessed our family with yet a *third* healthy pregnancy. This time, He gifted us with a girl.

These two experiences of loss could have easily led me to blame God for the heartache I endured. For isn't this what Satan hopes to accomplish through tragedy: turning one against God? But, what had happened was quite the opposite. God graciously allowed me to be tested in *my* weakness so He could build me up in *His* strength. I see very clearly now how God has utilized these tragic events to reveal so much about Himself to me through His unfaltering love and care. He was never going to let me fall because He knew His grace would be sufficient for me to come out triumphantly on the other side. Though I had thought what I needed in my life prior to these events could be found here on this earthly-world through man-led means, I was faced with the reality that all I truly and honestly need is *Him*.

I have learned a great deal through these experiences, but there is so much more that our Lord has to teach me. I am by no means finished with my journey, for it will be a life-long one. However, I hope and pray that I will have the courage and strength to trust in God's love every step of the way.

> *"Remember that I have commanded you to be determined and confident! Do not be afraid or discouraged, for I, the Lord your God, am with you wherever you go." (Joshua 1:9 GNT)*

Jacquelyn Scott

3

God is Mercy

"Our prayer and God's mercy are like two buckets in a well; while the one ascends the other descends."

– *Mark Hopkins*

My Atheist Husband

I met Craig, an internationally known dance instructor, in 1985 and became his dance partner. Twelve years later we married, and he became the step-father to my two children. Throughout our relationship it became very apparent that dancing was the only thing that I had in common with this quiet retired Lieutenant Colonel from the U.S. Army Corps of Engineers dance instructor who was a modest recipient of a Bronze Star, Purple Heart, and Meritorious Service Medal, just to name a few.

To compound our differences, I am a practicing Catholic whereas Craig was hostile towards the Catholic Church and the idea of religion in general. I attribute this hostility towards religion to his family background. It is not uncommon for a man who has had an unhealthy relationship with his father to have difficulty relating to God the Father. Craig was a classic example. These feelings of animosity towards religion were so strong that Craig was unable to even look at a religious piece of art in the house (even if he hung it on the wall for me), and any discussions we had about faith (which were rare) ended in a high degree of conflict. For example, I remember one particular family-group conversation that my Mom was involved in, discussing the existence of God. During this discussion, Craig stood up angrily, called my Mom "Ma-am" and Our Lord "Mr. Christ," and stormed out.

Craig's philosophy was that of an objectivist, but he had qualities that trumped the atheism he professed. He was honorable, honest, fair, and generous (particularly with my kids). Anyone who knew Craig recognized his generosity. He was generous with the time he dedicated to his students, both adults and children alike. He was extraordinarily generous with the time and money he spent on events with the swing-dance community. Craig was always there for my family, and he expressed his love for us through that generosity. My daughter, Tara, summed it up well by saying that a generous heart is a gift from God, and if you use that gift, it is impossible not to recognize God in the end.

Well, two years after we married I became even more serious about my Catholic faith, which I am sure was something Craig had not counted on when we had said our vows. However, it was important to Craig that I was happy, and so he willingly cooperated, supported, and respected all that was required in our sacramental marriage.

Although he was cooperative in our marital commitment, Craig was very difficult to live with. I relied completely on my faith, the Sacraments, and Our Lady's help to maintain harmony because I knew that pleases Our Lord. Craig was a lone-ranger type, and it was in his nature to hang on to his own control of every aspect of his life. He did not have good personal communication skills. He also carried a lot of anger internally and silently.

I honestly don't think he understood or recognized the gift of love until the day of his mother's funeral. He was blown away at the number of family members, friends, acquaintances, and former neighbors who came to pay their respects. It was incredible for me to witness the emotions he felt over the turnout at the funeral because Craig was such an introverted person.

Sometime later we were at a family event in Maryland where Craig and my son, Josh, stood next to each other looking out over the crowd gathered for a Thanksgiving celebration. Craig said to Josh, "So your Grandmother has created all of this." Josh said "yes," and all my husband could say was "wow." While Craig always knew that he was a part of our family, I think that he was beginning to appreciate the scope of the love of which he was a part.

In 2004 doctors diagnosed Craig with a debilitating neurological disease called corticobasal ganglionic degeneration, which affected his speech and ability to dance and walk. He ultimately and very quickly became bedridden. The remarkable thing about his progression of the disease is that his personality traits softened rather than turned harsher. It is common to see people who are ill become despondent or frustrated by their illness; this never happened with Craig. He was still extremely focused on himself, but he accepted his incapacities, became jovial over them, and even child-like in his acceptance. Amazingly Craig agreed to join me in the Eucharistic Adoration chapel for the duration that he was mobile on his portable scooter. It took some time for him to be comfortable and even peaceful there, but it happened. He also agreed to sit with us during the family Rosary, and even though he was probably working on something else during the prayers, he was still there with us. During his bed-ridden stage, —being "locked up in bed" as he would call it—I point-blank told him what to expect and what to say when he met Our Lord, a kind of Catholicism 101. He would dutifully nod his head in concurrence. There are no atheists in foxholes.

In the last few days of his life, Craig was agreeable to having the Rosary or the Divine Mercy Chaplet said at his bedside. He was allowed to receive the anointing of the sick and last rites of the Catholic Church since he was a veteran dying at a military medical facility, which I considered a tremendous gift from God. Josh, Tara, and I surrounded him at the end of his dying process. My sister, Annie, was with us; Josh's wife, Leah, arrived shortly before Craig died (we sincerely felt that he waited for her). His eyes were opened as his breathing became slower and slower. His head was tilted and his mouth was wide open as he took each breath. I was lying on the bed with him, caressing his face, saying short prayers for him, and expressing my love and joy for his going to meet Our Lord, which caused his moaning to stop. During the last hour of his life, I whispered prayers and "I love you's" to him. His breathing slowed, and he died. I whispered to him, "Lucky you Dink, now *you* know".

We witnessed an amazing sight a few moments after it was clear he passed away. I felt movement in his arm, his head turned straight, his mouth closed, and formed a most radiant smile. His open eyes were a beautiful blue. I never saw such a natural beautiful smile on him. There was "movement" as if his spirit left his body and he was meeting Our Lord. Then his head and face went back to the same position when he took his last breath. It was a beautiful thing to see, and I believe that it was his reaction to seeing the source of all of the love that had surrounded him throughout his life. Our Lord chose to give us a confirmation of Craig's salvation, despite his years of hostility towards religion. I believe He wanted to let us know He ultimately captured Craig's attention and soul.

Through this journey I accompanied with Craig, I'm awe-struck at the privilege of playing a part in his salvation without setting out to convert him. Although I didn't see it for the majority of the twenty-two years I knew Craig, I now have a better recognition of Our Lord actively working through ordinary events—and how mysteriously He uses us in His plan of salvation.

Though I did not have an ideal marriage, we did have a sacramental marriage as well as the commitment that is required of love. I wasn't even sure I loved Craig many-a-day, but I can say with complete certitude that I love and appreciate him now more than ever. Our Lord knew what He was doing all along. He had slowly been building a foundation for my mathematically-minded, rational, engineer husband, knowing that Craig would ultimately respond to a simple invitation.

In hindsight, I realize that Craig and I were actually very well suited for each other, which is pretty comical to think about now. I am grateful to Our Lord for the privilege of playing a part in Craig's salvation. Craig was like a closed castle door, but instead of opening to the simple pull of a chain, he responded to the open invitation of love. It really is true that the great theological virtue is Love and it is the only one that lasts. Truly awesome.

Lucy Renzi with Josh Renzi

Lead Us Not...

It wasn't until the death of my grandfather when I was twenty-six-years-old that I realized there had been a good Catholic role model in my family. It's a life changing experience when someone you've known your whole life dies, only to find out at their funeral that there was so much more to them—so much good that you never knew or cared to ask about.

My Catholic upbringing was not atypical, but it wasn't anything spiritually spectacular. My parents brought my siblings and me to Mass on Christmas, Easter, and some random days in between. They sent us to religious education classes, but even though I was in attendance, I was never fully engaged. By the time I was confirmed I wasn't prepared to appreciate the importance of this sacrament and instead found my life, like many other teenagers, lacking in faith and spiraling into a world filled with temptation that would ultimately lead to addiction. Fortunately, certain events in my life would free me from the vices of addiction and open my heart to experience the endless love and mercy of Christ.

Most people experience an addiction of some kind during their life. Different addictions can have different consequences, but they all involve the irresistible temptation to continue the habit. It's a scary thing when you can't physically stop yourself from doing something even when it stands against reason. Whether the addiction is food, sex, drugs, alcohol, TV, reading, pornography, gossip, negativity, or any other temptation, it grips you, occupies your mind, hijacks your body, and forces its persistent existence into every waking day. I dealt with my own addictions, like so many others do, and I found myself on a path of mental, physical, and spiritual destruction.

I'm not exactly sure when the first night terror happened, but I do know I experienced them at the height of my addictions. I was being attacked in my dreams and I didn't know by who, why or how. In each dream, I was always in the bed of the actual room where I was sleeping, unable to tell if I was awake or asleep when a dark, indistinguishable figure would slowly move towards me. Paralyzed, I would always be unable to move or speak. In my bed at home the figure strangled me: I couldn't breathe, and

I woke up gasping for air. In a hotel room I felt myself levitating off the bed, unable to move or stop myself from raising towards the figure; I was struggling to wake-up and somehow escaped harm at the last moment. Another time while I was taking a nap in my dorm room, I dreamt that I was laying on my left side with my right arm dangling over the edge of the bed. The dark figure was walking slowly across the room towards me. Again, I was paralyzed as the figure was reaching out his hand towards me, but just before he reached me a voice whispered in my ear, "Pull back." I immediately woke-up and realized I was in my dorm room bed, laying on my left side with my right arm dangling over the edge. The only difference between the dream and being awake was the absence of the dark figure in the room. Unaware of the reason or the cause, the dreams persisted.

The lack of a solid spiritual foundation in my youth was taking its toll on me during my college years. I found myself desiring faith in anything and searching for answers in all the wrong places. At the time, I was in a serious relationship with a girl who was Jewish and found myself contemplating a life content with studying Judaism.

My relationship with this girl had lasted the better part of two years and not without its issues. It seemed over time we were growing further and further apart and neither one of us knew when the right time was to quit. Then, one day standing outside our dorm building, she told me that she didn't want to raise her kids with a father who wasn't Jewish. In a moment of clarity, I realized that based on my childhood and my upbringing, I felt culturally Catholic. I told her that I grew-up Catholic and I couldn't erase that part of myself. It was at this critical moment in my life when things started culminating towards the answers I had been seeking; prayers were being heard that my mind didn't know my heart had been praying. While this was not an enlightening moment of faith per say, it was a necessary knock at the door that was waiting to be opened.

After mutually ending our relationship, I used my newly found freedom to live the "single-college-life", which meant I spent more time engaging in self-destructive habits. This was a dangerous time of over-confidence, a sense of invincibility, and inevitable risk-taking. The night terrors persisted in conjunction with my addictive tendencies, and I found myself caring less about others, myself, and the consequences of my actions. While at the time I felt I was at a high point in life, it was unknowingly to me a very low point. What happened next was the catalyst I needed to change for the better. Spoiler alert: she would be the woman I was going to marry.

Jackie came from a solid Catholic upbringing. She went to a Catholic grade school and high school and had countless role models within her very large, tight-knit family. When we met, we were at an interesting point in both of our lives. Jackie, a practicing Catholic all of her life, had recently stopped attending weekly Mass due to the conflict of emotions she was experiencing as a result of her own personal struggles, and, as previously shared, I had been struggling to find a faith of my own since I never fully committed myself to Catholicism.

Together one night, we watched a movie based on a true story involving the demonic possession of a young girl and the attempts to perform an exorcism on her. The girl in this movie was often attacked at night during which her body contorted from the evil possession. The other characters found themselves being attacked for their attempts to free the girl from her demons. I became intensely afraid, as the events of this story caused me to reflect on the night terrors I had been experiencing. Though I knew I was not possessed, I began thinking: *Are these dreams or are they demons? Why is this happening? What do I do? How can I…?* And then it dawned on me. I turned to Jackie and said, "I want to go to church."

That Sunday Jackie and I went to Mass, and we continued to attend regularly. For the first time in my life, I paid attention at Mass and there was substance to the readings and messages being relayed. I could feel the bond between Jackie and me growing stronger and I found myself looking forward to attending Mass with Jackie each week. We soon found that the more we involved God within our relationship, the closer and more connected we became. We openly talked with one another about our backgrounds in the Catholic faith. We prayed together, sought religious counsel together, and grew closer to God together. As I opened my heart more and more to God, there was less temptation to fall into my addictions. And, while difficult to avoid the *feeling* of temptation, over time I was eventually able to resist engaging in the *acts* that were preceded by temptation. Not only was I freed from the chains of my addictions, but the night terrors stopped the moment I started going to church and I haven't had one since.

Through my own personal struggle, I have come to learn that faith is a journey. Like any journey, there is a starting point and there is a destination. Along the way, there may be hills, potholes, traffic, flat tires, accidents, or anything else that will try to slow you down or stop you from getting to where you are going. Though my journey of faith has many miles left to travel, I am thankful that Christ has led me to the starting point and equipped me with the courage and desire to continue.

If there is one thing I can leave you with, it is to encourage you to not allow your temptations, addictions, or any other personal qualms to keep you from starting or continuing with your own journey of faith. God's love and mercy is endless. I have experienced it in my life, and more than anything, He wants you to know the healing power of it in yours.

Lead us not into temptation, but deliver us from evil.

Brad M. Scott

Thank Heaven for Kevin

Our son, Kevin, was born August 22, 1991 in Evansville, Indiana. There were no complications during the pregnancy, so we had every expectation that he would be born perfectly healthy, like his sister, Marisa, who was born two years earlier.

Kevin entered the world at 6:47pm on a Thursday evening. Almost immediately I noticed the doctor looking with concern at the nurse who was assisting him with the delivery. I looked at my son and noticed a lump at the top of his head covered by a tuft of hair. The medical team carried out its normal post-birth routine and within a few minutes my wife, Leslie, was holding our son not aware that there was a serious problem.

I went downstairs to eat dinner in the hospital cafeteria. As I finished eating I heard the hospital public address system paging me to immediately go to Leslie's room. When I arrived I found Leslie crying while talking to the delivery nurse. Standing nearby in a coat and tie was a distinguished looking young gentleman. He was a pediatric neurosurgeon.

"What's the problem?" I asked. The doctor told me that Kevin was born with a spinal meningocele, a hernial protrusion of the meninges through a defect in the cranium. This is a very rare birth defect affecting about one in twenty-five thousand births in the United States. The doctor explained that surgery would be necessary to prevent brain damage. If left untreated, he said, a spinal meningocele continues to grow preventing the skull from closing resulting in potentially serious brain damage.

Needless to say, I was stunned. I asked the doctor whether he had ever performed this kind of surgery. "No, I have not; however, I am familiar with the procedure as I observed such an operation in medical school," he responded.

My immediate reaction was that we must put Kevin in the care of a pediatric neurosurgeon who had *experience* with the kind of surgery he needed. To my disappointment, the doctor was indignant and argued his case to perform the surgery in Evansville.

A few days later we walked into the office of Dr. Leland Albright, head of pediatric neurosurgery at Children's Hospital in Pittsburgh. I will never forget that one of the first things I noticed were pictures on a wall of what seemed like hundreds of healthy, smiling babies and toddlers Dr. Albright had operated on over the years.

After a short wait we were ushered into an examining room and were soon greeted by Dr. Albright. In his early to mid-fifties Dr. Albright was a tall man, soft-spoken and seemed to be very sensitive about our concern, or more accurately, our fear. He explained that the removal of the meningocele could be rather easy, or it could be problematic. After explaining what he would do during the surgery, he gently took Kevin from Leslie and held him in his huge hands and looked at Kevin's face for several seconds. Then he looked up at us and smiled and said reassuringly, "Everything will be okay."

We returned to Pittsburgh a couple of weeks later for an MRI that would hopefully provide Dr. Albright and his team with a clear picture of the meningocele. Unfortunately, the MRI revealed that it extended deeper into the brain than previously thought.

The next two weeks before Kevin's surgery were very difficult. While we had confidence in Dr. Albright, we were advised that there was a real possibility that the surgery could result in brain damage to our son. Every day before work I went to 7:00am Mass to pray for our son.

We arrived at Children's Hospital about two hours before surgery was scheduled to begin. After about an hour a nurse came and took Kevin to pre-op. A few minutes later I noticed several young men and women in white coats walking past us toward the surgery area. About thirty minutes before the scheduled start of the surgery at 1:00pm, a nurse approached us with papers to sign giving permission for more than a dozen medical interns to observe the surgery.

We expected the operation to last at least two hours and, as best as we could, tried to steel ourselves for the possibility of bad news. As I was nervously pacing up and down the hallway about a half an hour after the surgery began, I suddenly saw Dr. Albright approaching me. I thought that something must have gone wrong. As he approached me the good doctor broke out in a reassuring grin as he guided me over to where Leslie was sitting and said, "The surgery is over. The tissue was positioned in such a way that it was relatively easy to remove, and I did not even have to touch his brain."

We were stunned at such unexpected wonderful news. "How long will Kevin be in the hospital," Leslie asked. Dr. Albright smiled and said, "You can take him home later this afternoon!"

As we walked across the street to a nearby restaurant for some lunch we hardly said a word to one another. I think that we were almost in shock over how everything turned out so well, so quickly. About half way through lunch I saw tears of relief on Leslie's face. Later the next day, while we were sitting around the kitchen table at Leslie's parents' house, surrounded by a very grateful family, I could not take my eyes off Kevin as Leslie held him with his head completely wrapped in a white bandage that covered most of his head. I repeatedly thanked the Good Lord for answering our prayers.

Today, Kevin is a perfectly healthy, strong young man. The scar on his head is just slightly visible. Perhaps it's a permanent reminder of how fortunate we are that God answered our prayers twenty-two years ago.

Mike Deshaies

My Spiritual Journey

My spiritual journey is long and varied. I was born into a family with a strong Catholic faith and deep roots in the Church. But sometime during my thirteenth year, my mom stopped practicing our religion and therefore I did too. We stopped attending Mass; I rarely prayed. I didn't see evidence of God in the world because I didn't look for Him. I still don't know why my mother stopped attending Mass. Church hadn't seemed important to her for a while, and I never questioned her choice. Church seemed boring to me as a child, so I just accepted her decision without question of why weekly Mass attendance was no longer required of the two of us.

To be honest, I was relieved to not have to attend church anymore. I was a kid who wanted to spend my time hanging out with friends or playing video games, not sitting on a hard pew listening to a priest talk about things I didn't understand. I did so many terrible things during that time away from my faith: skipping school, sneaking out at night, drinking, and running away from home. More than once, my mother tried to convince the state to put me in foster care or a psychiatric hospital. She was that desperate to control my behavior. It didn't ever occur to me that I could pray and ask for help, or even that God cared about what I was doing.

I didn't know it at the time, but even though I'd given up on God, He hadn't given up on me. He sent help in the form of my Aunt Annie and my grandmother. Aunt Annie took me in and saved me from becoming a ward of the state; my grandmother showed me unconditional, but nonetheless tough, love. The two of them each took one of my hands, slapped them together, and taught me to pray.

Unfortunately, their efforts took several years to pay off. I continued to suffer from what I call spiritual laziness. I just didn't try to have a relationship with God. When people think about a "spiritual experience," most of them probably imagine a sudden transformation resulting from a concrete, observable event. For me the transformation was gradual. I can't pinpoint a time when it happened, except to say that the Holy Spirit called me a little louder each day until I could no longer ignore Him.

One day, during my first year in college, I walked into the local Catholic parish that was closest to my apartment at the time. The church was holding confessions for the Sacrament of Reconciliation; nobody was in line, so I walked right into the confessional. I said, "Bless me, Father, for I have sinned. It has been a really long time since my last confession." I started to explain where I'd been for the past several years, but I couldn't begin to remember all of my sins. The priest was so happy that I was there. He suggested I contact a woman at the parish about something he called "The Sacrament of Remembering," which was supposed to be for Catholics who'd fallen away from the Church and wanted to come back. "Remembering" is not one of the regular seven sacraments, and I've never heard of it outside of that conversation, but his suggestion intrigued me. I wish I'd called that woman, but I never did. I still wonder what would've happened if I did. I'm so glad I walked into that confessional, though. It was an enormous relief to not only be forgiven for my sins, but to have this priest sit there and not just tell me, but really *show* me through his joyful reaction that I was welcome in the Church, and I really did belong there. I still wasn't quite ready to fully commit myself to God, but I did start attending Mass sporadically.

I let life and busyness get in the way of fully practicing my faith for a few years. It was as if I was starting to feel that God should be part of my life, but I hadn't fully accepted it yet.

But eventually, I went back to Mass. Eventually, I prayed the Rosary. Eventually, I read the Scriptures. Not every day or every week at first, but that happened eventually too. Now prayer is such an integral part of my life that I can't imagine a day without it. I've used it to share joy and to ask for help.

I had a lot of tough days when I was pregnant with my third child. My body ached; my nerves were fried from wrangling two small children all day every day; and of course, the hormones sent my emotions reeling. I was frequently on the edge of losing my temper with the kids, or my husband, or even any well-meaning person who asked how I was doing.

So I prayed. Every day, especially if I felt like I was having difficulties with the kids, I asked for help from Our Blessed Mother. Several times I asked her, "Would you be their mother today? I'm not doing my best." I think Mary knew that my children needed my love, in addition to her own, so she took care of me. She gave me peace so that I could be their mother. I thank her for that, and I thank God for the kids.

This is where my spiritual journey is now. I've come a long way, and I know that it is far from over. I am by no means a perfect Catholic. (Is anyone?) I'm never able to concentrate on the Mysteries while I'm praying the Rosary. I sometimes devote less than five minutes to prayer in a day. I let stress overwhelm me and forget that I can turn to God for guidance. But I'm better at it than I was yesterday, and I hope to improve more tomorrow. I still need help, but at least now I know where to look for it.

Anonymous

To Be Continued

My story begins in July of 1950. It is one of a man who has truly been blessed by the grace of God—a story of God, faith, the love between a man and woman, and the suffering from alcohol and prescription medication addictions. It clearly shows the hand of God working in my life.

By telling my story I want God's love, grace and glory to shine through me for everyone to see and understand that Jesus is alive, although not seen in the physical form, still walking the earth today performing miracles all over the world, teaching the word of God through words and deeds, and that "faith"—even the size of a mustard seed—produces great results far beyond our scope of hope and imagination. It is my hope that readers of this story will not only come to know what "true love" is, but will feel it deep down in their hearts and souls, whether it be love for family, friends or that "special someone". I also hope that, once and for all, innocent people's lives may be able to be saved through the recognition of what a true, dedicated and committed doctor is and is not.

I was born on July 21, 1950 in Elkton, Maryland and raised in New Castle, Delaware. My parents were hard-working, loving and dedicated parents of modest means. I was an only child, not spoiled by any means, but taught about love, respect, morals, and values. I went to a Catholic school and was eventually placed in a public school where I did very well academically and socially. Life was good—the best childhood a kid could have: breakfast every morning, lunch every afternoon, and dinner was on the table at 6:00pm. There were vacations every summer at the beach, always accompanied by my Aunt Marie, Uncle Joe (my dad's brother), and my two cousins, Jim and Krista, who lived right next door. It was like having two mothers, two fathers, and a sister and brother. Life was great—seemingly all so simple as I look back to the "good ole days".

Following high school, I followed my childhood dream and went into radio broadcasting. After a very short stint in the Air National Guard, I got my first job as a disc jockey and later met my wife-to-be, who I married in June of 1973. At the time of our marriage she was just eighteen-years-old, five years my junior. Together we had two boys, Frank and Jess, who were three years apart. They were happy and healthy, typical American boys—thank God! I was heavily involved in raising them: sitting with them from the time they were three-months-old while my wife returned to work, being involved in all of their school activities, and coaching each boy in baseball and basketball for seventeen years. We went on family vacations to the beach every summer like I did as a child and once to Disney World. The boys got along as well as brothers do. The youngest, Jess, was a "spirited" soul, who got into "Leave It To Beaver" type of trouble, while Frank was more reserved.

The family, from an outsider's perspective, seemed to be the "perfect" family. But, behind closed doors it was a different world. My wife and I were having major trouble (at least in my eyes), which started even before the wedding. Reflecting back, I'm sad to say, I never loved her and after a while I doubted seriously that I was who she wanted to spend the rest of her life with. Although I tried very hard—remembering my vows to God and knowing through my Catholic upbringing that divorce was not an option—the difference in our cultures and upbringing were pushing us farther apart until we finally separated three months before our thirtieth wedding anniversary.

In October of 2003, our divorce was finalized and we each went our separate ways. The boys were twenty-six and twenty-three at the time and I believe they felt that the divorce was inevitable. After receiving the news, each son said to me, "Dad, we still love you both the same and we don't need to know what happened".

After selling our home, I bought a new house I had built right over the state line in the town where I was born. Frank had since graduated from college and was a college head soccer coach. He remains a head soccer coach with a major university and is quite successful with his career and as a family man: he is now a husband and a loving father of a boy and a girl.

Jess, on the other hand, had dropped out of college after attending for two years and was working odd jobs trying to "find" himself—the most loving and caring soul who walked the earth was "lost" and trying to find his "dream". He said to me one day, "Dad, all I want to do is get married and have kids". Unfortunately, he never did and never would: he died on June 5, 2007. That was truly the beginning of what looked like my end.

Finding my son dead in our home was the single biggest and most tragic event of my life! His death would alter the course of my life, forever. After finding him in his room that day, I proceeded to do what any normal father and person would do in this type of situation: I planned the funeral. After over a thousand mourners attended his funeral, I attempted to go on with my life as I knew it. But, I couldn't. After approximately five months, the realization that Jess was never coming home again set in and I had a nervous breakdown, crying and drinking heavily for three straight days. I ended up falling down a flight of stairs and almost died. I severely injured my shoulder by the fall for which I would need six operations. When my son Frank and my friend Bob finally found me, I was taken to the hospital and later to a rehab facility. That night my son and best friend were told, "He may not make it through the night". But, God had other plans for me.

Some weeks following that initial episode, I was coaxed by friends and family to seek the help of a psychiatrist to help me with my grief. I took their advice and saw a doctor, who just after five minutes of meeting me in his office and learning of my son, asked me, "What kind of pills do you want?" I was shocked! I had no idea what he was talking about and told him so. He then prescribed something and scheduled a follow-up appointment. This was *not* what I expected nor wanted! But, I took the medicine in hopes of it calming me down a little. I came back a week or so later for a follow-up visit and he never even discussed my problem with me. It was then that I decided to find another doctor. After consulting with my family doctor, I was referred to someone else.

I made the appointment with the new doctor and really liked him. He was elderly, spoke with a Spanish accent, had receding white hair, wore glasses, sported a small white beard and mustache, looked neatly trimmed, and was short and portly in stature. He seemed to be very friendly and thorough, asking me what brought me to him and then proceeded to outline, somewhat, what he was going to do in subsequent appointments. He asked me a lot of questions about my childhood, parents, family life, my marriage, my children, etc. During the next two or three visits, he asked me questions about who the president was when I was born, current political events, etc. I guess he was trying to determine if I was of sound mind. He also prescribed more medications, such as antidepressants, anti-anxiety meds, sleeping pills, and more. This was the start of more than four years of an exorbitant, almost deadly amount of pill consumption—pills that nearly killed me and caused side-effects that made me suicidal, have bouts of uncontrolled anger, fits of crying, etc. When things didn't seem to be getting better with me, he would either change my meds or increase the strength/dosage. I was seeing him weekly while under his care, but not getting any better. He and I had seemingly become friends and at one point he even asked if I would come to his home to help him with his computer. During the course of my care, he had disclosed much of his personal life to me: his life in his native country, his career, his marriage, his finances, his love for other women, his divorces, and his failing health. On two separate occasions he had asked if he could prescribe Cymbalta in my name, which he was taking himself, so I could fill it and bring the pills back to him.

Though I was having weekly visits with him, I was not getting any better with my grief and was diagnosed with Post Traumatic Stress Disorder (PTSD) and put on 100% disability. At this point in time my friends were beginning to shy away from me and I from them. They would offer help such as advising me to get a new doctor, telling me to get off "those pills", stop drinking, etc. I was ignoring everything that was important in my life—family, friends, church, and my home.

In December of 2012, not long after seeing this doctor weekly for about three years, I met Becky. After our initial meeting, Becky and I spent Christmas Day with my family of aunts and cousins. I fell in love with Becky, knowing and telling her she was an angel from heaven sent by God. During the course of our relationship, she would teach me what real love is about and how it feels. I knew then, as I do now, that God placed her in my life to take care of me in my darkest moments and to open up my mind, body and soul to God's grace and goodness.

In March of 2013, we got engaged on her birthday. It was on this day that I began to spiral on a rapid decline that would traumatize Becky beyond belief. During this decline, I was re-committed to rehab facilities, I wrecked my car which nearly killed me at the scene and put me in a coma for two days, and even more! Needless to say, the year we were engaged was both the happiest and ugliest year.

It seemed I would lose control every two months. In between my uncontrollable, terrifying outbreaks was the most loving and beautiful time of our lives. Becky knew, however, that these episodes of horror were caused by the tremendous amounts of prescribed pills I was taking coupled with my drinking of alcohol. She called my psychiatrist and expressed her concerns about the outbreaks and side effects of all the medications. Whatever was said during that conversation left her very angry with him. She told me that she believed it was my medications causing these outbreaks and I should talk to my doctor about stopping them. I did talk to him about it and I will never forget his response. He said, "No, you are going to be sick the rest of your life, you need these pills". Contrary to the doctor's instructions, I tried to stop taking the medication several times. However, whenever I would attempt weaning myself off all of the meds I would feel really strange. Each attempt to stop taking the pills would last for about four days and then I would start taking them again thinking that the strange feelings were a result of my PTSD, not of withdrawal. Sometimes I would take more than was prescribed in order to help me feel better again. It was a vicious cycle.

Twice Becky had me committed to a hospital to get me off of the medications. I stayed in the hospital for about a week each time I was committed and was almost completely weaned off all of the pills. When I was released both times, I was instructed to follow-up with my doctor. I did and he proceeded to tell me that I needed those pills and then prescribed more, saying again, I was going to be sick for the rest of my life. In addition to all of the medications he prescribed me over the years, I was taking a lot of pain medications as a result of my numerous shoulder surgeries to repair my rotator cuff from that previous fall down the stairs. I had six surgeries in six years. I was stuck in a vicious merry-go-round of pills and alcohol. I trusted my doctor, believed in him, and thought he was my friend and would help me. But, he refused to listen to the concerns of Becky and he either did not see or totally ignored my uncontrollable actions that were caused by the side effects of the medications. Finally, this seemingly endless cycle came to a standstill on December 20, 2013.

The night of December 19, 2013, I started another one of the horrifying episodes over, of all things, a fishing pole. What happened that night is not clear, fuzzy to say the least. I recall the usual threats of suicide, holding a knife to my chest and screaming and crying. I remember standing in the doorway between the master bedroom and the pool while I was drinking a bottle of wine that I had apparently gotten from the wine rack in the kitchen. The next thing I remember was waking up the following morning alone. And, that was my last drink of alcohol for the rest of my life.

Then, there was another time when the details of the day's events were once again unclear. I don't remember when it was, how long it had been, but I was in *jail*! My earliest recollections are mere flashbacks and I can't attest to their validity. I recall waking up in a jail cell with other guys: I was scared—fearful of being beaten and raped. I felt lost, frightened, like I had never felt before and completely helpless. I no longer had any control over my life. My life was in somebody else's hands and there was nothing I could do about it.

While I was incarcerated, I was having constant hallucinations, horrifying nightmares, and paranoia. I was talking to the walls, hiding under beds, seeing and hearing things and people that weren't there and feeling lost, helpless—like I was going to die. A lot of times I truly wanted to die because I thought dying would be better than what I was experiencing—withdrawal from alcohol and prescription medication. But, dying then was not in God's plan for me.

I vividly remember, and will never forget, one day during my withdrawal when I was laying on my back, seemingly on a stretcher or gurney of some type. I recall my head violently shaking and moving rapidly from side to side, spewing saliva everywhere. I was cold. Someone was yelling to me to open my eyes, just for a second. When I finally did open them I saw lights so bright I had to close them immediately. I heard someone else say something about how they brought me "back" once. Then, somebody said, "Put the paddles on his chest in case we need them again." My eyes remained tightly closed. I heard a man's voice say "Damn, that girl is a saint." It was then I knew Becky was there, physically or spiritually! A man's voice said "I can't believe he is alive with a blood alcohol content of 0.50, most people die at 0.40." He said over and over that he couldn't believe it. Then someone else said I only had four-beats-per-minute and to let me lie there and I would eventually "go off". I then remember someone rubbing my chest really hard. It hurt really badly. Then, someone catheterized me, a pain so bad I will never forget it. Moments later somebody said, "Drive him by his fiancé's house so he can see it one last time before he goes."

The next thing I knew, I was lying down in the back of a pickup truck riding slowly by Becky's house. All this time I wanted the last words on my lips before I died to be "I love Becky". I kept repeating these words over and over. By this time, I knew I was dying. I looked for the "light', but there was none. I thought there had to be a light, but there wasn't one. Then I looked in the upper right hand corner of my eye and I saw and heard something I will never forget as long as I live. There, on a white horse, was a man dressed in a suit of armor holding a long spear. He said to me in a loud voice, "Do you want to fight this battle?" I immediately thought that was Jesus and said "Yes, Jesus, I can't lose with you." I don't remember anything after that until I woke-up sometime towards the end of February 2014. When I realized where I was and somewhat about what was happening, I remembered the vision of the man on the white horse—to me Jesus—and it was then I knew my life was no longer in anybody's hands but God's. At that moment I turned my life over to God. I realized I could not do anything without God and that nothing is impossible for Him. I then realized what the true meaning of faith is: "[...] the assurance of things hoped for, the conviction of things not seen" (Hebrews 11:1 New American Standard Bible).

The rest of my time in jail, I fought very hard to get my memory working by keeping track of the time, day, month and year. I practiced by remembering everything about Becky, our time together and how much I loved her and missed her. I practiced remembering song titles and artists, the year the songs came out, old phone numbers, and friend's names and addresses. I kept getting stronger each day, more confident the day would come when I would be released and be back with Becky. I read the Bible twice, went to church services, and attended Bible studies that were conducted in the cell. I prayed with other inmates. I read books, played cards, watched TV and slept a lot. All I could think about was Becky. I loved her, missed her and cared for her. I worried about her, felt devastated by what I had done to her.

Then on the morning of May 14, 2014, I was taken to court. I was transported to the courthouse alone, without any other inmates, as was the norm. After the twenty-minute ride we arrived at the courthouse where I met with my attorney in the hallway. I had asked if everything was still in place—the agreement between the prosecutor and us that would allow all my charges to be dismissed and allow me to go free. I was told sternly by my attorney, "No, things have changed." Confused, I asked her what she meant by that. All she said was that I had to plead "no contest". When I asked what that meant, she abruptly replied that it meant I wasn't pleading "guilty" but I wasn't pleading "not guilty". It would show up on my record as "adjudicated guilty". She then hurriedly went through some instructions for me to follow while in the courtroom.

When we finally entered the courtroom, it was empty, dimly lit, cold and eerie. Moments later a couple of men in suits carrying brief cases entered along with a police officer or two. That was all. My attorney walked over to talk to one of the men and then disappeared into a side room for a few minutes. When she returned to where I was standing—at a podium with a microphone—she asked me if I had any questions and if I knew what to say. I was scared, but I nodded *yes* and waited. Silence fell over the courtroom and seconds later a male voice bellowed out, "Please stand…" After a preliminary exchange was given between those in attendance, the judge, as if he were in a hurry, started reading my charges, instructions and other things to me, stopping momentarily only to ask if I understood what he was saying. When he was finished, he read each charge again and asked how I pleaded. I said "no contest" to each. After all the charges were read, he proceeded to read something else which was hard to hear and understand. The next thing I knew he was getting up and leaving the courtroom. When he left, papers were quickly exchanged and signed. I was brought to the front of the courtroom by one of the police officers and was swabbed for DNA. While this was taking place, most of the others had left. When I was finished I walked back over to my attorney who handed me a paper and we talked for a minute. Then, she left, not to be seen by me ever again. I was then taken back to jail where I awaited my release.

Around 3:00pm that day I was taken out of my cell and moved to a cell in the Booking Area, where I was released about forty-five minutes later. I was dressed in the clothes given to me: hospital scrubs, a pair of hospital socks and a green striped polo shirt that was mine. I also received a piece of cardboard that was laminated, which contained my wallet, and much to my surprise, my wedding ring Becky had bought me for our wedding day. After my release I took a cab to a nearby Hampton Inn, where my friend Bob had made reservations for me the day before in anticipation of my release. When I arrived at the front desk I was scared and my mind was in a "fog". But, I was so happy to regain my freedom, the freedom I had lost for almost five months. The clerk behind the desk, Tia, was a middle-aged woman with long dark hair and a smile. She asked, "Can I help you?" I was a total mess physically, sporting a three-day beard, uncombed hair, and clothes that looked like they had been run over by a truck. I smiled back and gave her my information. She gave me the key-card to my room. Feeling ashamed and embarrassed, I quickly apologized for my unkempt appearance and quietly explained to her from where I just had come. She was very nice, welcomed me to the hotel and said a few kind words. I then went to my room to shower and shave and put on some new clothes that I had bought at a nearby department store before I arrived at the hotel.

That day was the beginning of what has since become a wonderful friendship, not only with Tia, but with her husband and her whole family, including her grandchildren. It was also the start of my "new life", a life that to this day is filled with happiness, a new, stronger faith in God, family and friends, and a start of a new faith in myself. For the first time I have learned to reflect on my life, as I had done many times during the months of my incarceration. And, I learned once again something I guess I always knew but never admitted—that I felt I was truly a good person. I now love myself for who I am and forgave myself for what I had done. I realized it was now time to take care of *me*—for if I didn't, I couldn't take care of anyone else. I had to take care of *myself* first. And, I know that one day Becky will take me back and we will once again be together. God hasn't brought me this far to abandon me.

Now I am working towards putting the pieces of my life back together while placing everything in God's hands. I can only do so much, the rest I've turned over to God. Life has many chapters; one bad chapter doesn't mean it's the end of the book. Reflecting back on the painful experience of losing my son, I can see that instead of it being the end, it turned out to be the beginning of the most spiritual, uplifting, eye-opening, and life-saving periods of my sixty-five years. I have never felt stronger, better, smarter, wiser, or more happy and spiritual in all of my life. God stepped in and took control. If it weren't for God and God placing Becky in my life, I would not be here to write this today. He, through Becky, saved my life at least five times during those seven years of living in a deep dark black hole. I am here for a reason—maybe it's to write this story to help others learn from my experiences with faith, love, doctors, alcohol, and prescription medicines. One thing is for sure, this story is being shared to show how God's glory and grace shines through what He has done for me. And, I know He has much more in store for my life, which is why this story is entitled, "To Be Continued".

Francis L. Kulas, Jr.

The Power of Prayer

It was a Thursday morning in May, two months after I had given birth to my first child. I had just taken a much needed shower (a simple luxury at the time) and was enjoying the brief time I had to myself. As I was getting ready for the day, I caught a glimpse in the mirror of a black spot on my back. I knew I had a flesh-colored mole on my back and was immediately concerned. I called for my husband and asked him to take a look at the mole. He said that yes, there was indeed a black spot on it. He took a picture of the mole so I could get a better look.

The first thought that came into my head after reviewing the picture was, "Melanoma!" I had tanned a lot (both indoor and outdoor exposure) throughout my junior and senior year of high school, and even during college, so I knew that I was at an increased risk for skin cancer. But, I never in a million years would have thought I would develop the deadlier form of skin cancer: melanoma! My mind started racing, and my thoughts went directly to my little baby; I didn't want anything to happen to me because I now had a precious child to care for.

I decided that the next step I needed to take was to schedule an appointment with the dermatologist as soon as possible so I could have the mole evaluated. When I called the dermatologist, the receptionist informed me that the next available appointment was in August. August was three months away! If the spot on my mole was indeed melanoma, then I didn't have the luxury of time on my side.

Well, I went ahead and scheduled the August appointment since it was the earliest availability, and I did not want to risk having to wait even longer if I did not take it. Still not feeling comfortable with the distant date of the appointment, I called back and explained the urgency of my request to see the dermatologist. As a result, I was able to schedule an earlier appointment in June.

After getting off of the phone with the dermatologist's office, I found myself engrossed with the fear of melanoma. I cried to my husband, who comforted me and told me that it was all going to be okay. His rational nature encouraged me not to jump to conclusions prior to the dermatologist's evaluation. Unfortunately, when you have a black spot that has spontaneously appeared on one of your moles, it is difficult to not think about the possibility of skin cancer, especially when everything on the internet has already confirmed it to be melanoma.

In the meantime, my husband and I decided to pray the Chaplet of Divine Mercy Novena, asking Jesus to heal me of any skin cancer. I called my parents to tell them of the discovery and asked them to please pray for me, as well.

As we started praying the novena, I found myself feeling less consumed with anxious thoughts and more focused on drawing strength from Jesus, which in turn brought peace into my heart. I knew that the only way I would be able to handle whatever I was about to face was if I had Jesus right by my side. He had said, "For where two or three come together in my name, I am there with them," (Matthew 18:20 GNT). Between my husband and my parents, I already had a strong number of supporters praying on my behalf of this request. I trusted His words and relied on His promise throughout the novena.

Two days prior to my dermatology appointment I decided to look at the mole once more. As I turned my head to see it in the mirror, I couldn't find it. I tried to readjust my eyes, thinking I must have just missed it, but again there was no black spot to see. I called for my husband and asked him to take a look at the mole. He confirmed what I had seen; the black spot had disappeared. I was speechless. When I found my words, I said, "Jesus answered our prayers."

I called my mom and told her the good news. It was then that she had informed me that along with my dad and her, my brother and sister had joined in praying the novena too. I knew at that moment that Jesus had heard the prayers of a family who came together in His name and He lovingly and mercifully answered. Although the black spot had vanished before I had my appointment, I decided to keep the appointment because I was interested to see what the dermatologist would say about my disappearing black spot.

The day of the appointment had arrived, and as I was waiting for the dermatologist in the patient's room, I took out my digital camera that housed the evidence of the ominous "black spot." After the dermatologist came into the room and greeted me, I showed her the image that was taken three months prior. She looked at the picture and gasped, "That looks like melanoma." I'm sure she was wondering why I was showing her a picture instead of directing her to my back to examine the actual mole, so I then said, "Okay, now look at the mole on my back. Do you see any indication of the black spot that you just saw in the picture?" She examined the mole and said, "No, not at all." I continued with another question, "Is there any sign that there had been anything on the mole at all?" She again looked and said, "No, I don't see anything wrong with this mole. It looks completely fine."

I sat on the examination table beaming because I knew there was no other way to explain what had happened except that when my family went to Jesus in prayer, the black spot disappeared. I will never doubt the power of prayer.

Anonymous

Take this Porn and Shove It!

People these days talk about how hard it is to break the habits and/or addictions of drugs, gambling, and alcohol. These struggles have been around for so long that, unless it is affecting someone in your family, they are just brushed off. There are also a ton of places to seek help and information about these particular addictions. However, there is one addiction that has been around for a long time but has only just recently started surfacing. It is also probably the hardest one to break: pornography. Besides hunger, lust is probably our most primal instinct. And if it gets out of control, becoming rampant, you've got one hell of a fight on your hands! No pun intended because "Hell" is exactly what you're up against, trust me.

Between the ages of five and seven I was sexually abused, leading me into a life that literally revolved around porn. From this young age forward I was constantly bombarded with disturbing images, which I consider to be "spiritual warfare attacks" because there was no other reason for me to have these images in my mind. In fact, a lot of them were quite violent in nature. I may have only been five or six, but my thought-life would have made a war-hardened sailor blush.

You may wonder how a kid under seven-years-of-age knew about this kind of stuff. The only answer I can provide is that these thoughts could only be hell-born. I experienced these attacks throughout and beyond my childhood. Since I did grow up with these attacks during young childhood, I thought this was all a normal part of life, just not something you openly talked about. So, I didn't talk about it.

As time went on and I got older, I found out about real porn and, surprisingly, sources presented themselves to me on how to get it. However, the biggest contributor to my porn supply continued to be my own mind, my fantasies. I had the annoying ability to turn almost *any* image of a woman into something sexual in my head. I'm completely ashamed to admit it. Unfortunately, this mentality served my addiction over the years... an addiction that continued to strengthen and worsen.

After I got married, I discovered computers. Now, computers in and of themselves are wonderful tools but if improperly used can lead to disaster. I started by using the PC as an expensive gaming toy, but I eventually branched out and found out about bulletin board systems (BBS's), where I learned how to share adult pictures, programs, and text files. Eventually, I was able to interact with BBS's all over the world.

In time, I gained access to the internet. I honestly did not think of using the internet to look around for smut until a user/friend from my BBS told me about chat rooms and how I could find and trade adult pictures and video clips with other people while chatting live with women. This friend also showed me how to set up the software and where to find the smut. Plus, he showed me the places to stay out of because of the illegal content that they contained.

You would think that since I was married, a red flag would go up... but it didn't. This is when the hardcore building blocks to my personal hell and damnation really started, and I dragged my wife and son right along with me. Engaging in this lifestyle was like having an affair, which in God's eyes, it is. I describe this time in my life as if I got behind the wheel of a "porn car" with a warp drive switch on it; I was driving so fast that my guardian angel could not keep-up.

As I traded and chatted, usually with several people at once, I quickly (really quickly) built a large collection of pictures and videos. I also came across file names that indicated possible illegal content. So, I segregated the questionable files to another area on the PC to verify whether they were legal or illegal at a later time, while I deleted what I instantly deemed to be illegal. This behavior continued for about seven or eight years, and all the while I was not being the father or husband I should have been. The addiction, which was full-blown at this point, had taken complete control of me, my family life, and even my work life.

Eventually, my addiction led me into some of the illegal chat rooms I had initially avoided. I was scared to venture in these but rationalizing my impulses (and hormones) took over. I was careful at first, but while chatting with others in separate windows, I became too relaxed for my own good. I went out of control downloading and chatting, looking and even acting out (all the time avoiding my wife and son). I literally, and shamefully, "cybered" away my son's childhood. I am brought to tears quite often if I think about it too long.

Toward the end of this hell-ride, I told myself on several occasions that I had had enough, and in turn would destroy everything I owned that was porn-related: disks, CD's, DVD's, and all files on the hard drive. Each and every time I committed to ridding myself of the porn, I would find myself in front of the PC trading again within twenty-four hours. I never had the self-control to stay away from the temptation for more than a day at a time.

One day, when I was trading for an unusually long time, a strong feeling came over me. I experienced what I feel was a "divine conviction," or what some may call an epiphany. At this very moment, it became clear to me that something was horribly wrong: I was not being the husband and father who I was supposed to be. Rather, what I saw myself doing was something I did not like. My behavior was something very, very ugly, and I no longer wanted to engage in it. But, I did not know how to rid myself of it. I was suddenly very frightened.

I felt so guilty, remorseful, and dirty that I grabbed my crucifix down from the wall, fell to my knees next to my bed, literally sobbing, and did something I had never done before: I begged God for help. I asked him to take away the porn addiction; I didn't want it any more. I was at the point where I could no longer control my life, and I needed Him to take the wheel because I was stuck in a ditch.

Though I desperately wanted my addiction to end, I couldn't find the power within me to stop for more than one day at a time. It is nearly impossible to rid yourself in just one day of a lifestyle that has taken precedence for thirty-five years—a lifestyle that I chose to live because of my God-given free will. Then, *two weeks* after I *invited* God into my life, He opened the door to the resources it would take for me to regain my immortal soul from the grips of Satan.

On December 10, 2001 I was returning home from work with the full intent to trade, and when I saw my wife's car in the driveway I was disappointed. As I opened the front door, I saw that she was sitting on the edge of the sofa looking at me, oddly. I walked in and was surprised to see a county policeman standing in my living room. He said, "Mr. McDowell?" I replied, "Yes?" The policeman said that they had a warrant to search the house for child pornography.

The FBI and state police were confiscating all of my computers and camera equipment, including my son's (because I was the one who gave them to him). As it turned out, since I had become so relaxed with the trading I had not thoroughly filtered through all the files I traded. Unbeknownst to me, some illegal content was included in the mix of files that I had sent to an undercover university detective in Illinois and Maryland.

Consequently, I was asked if I would be willing to go to FBI headquarters for questioning. I said yes right away since I had no intention of lying. After ninety minutes of questioning, the FBI found nothing to hold against me. Our friend suggested we should hire an attorney due to the nature of the questioning, so my wife and I immediately hired a high-profile attorney who quickly told us not to answer any more questions from the police.

Nothing further happened for the next few *years*. The State and FBI said they held no charges against me but that the Assistant US Attorney did. At the time, I thought the Assistant US Attorney was bucking for a promotion, and it wasn't until much later that I found out he (mistakenly) thought I had some kind of connection with the mob in New York.

During this time, my wife and I had gone back to church for the first time in twenty years. I felt something was going on with the "Big Guy" upstairs because everything seemed to be too much like a test. So, I unofficially agreed (with myself) to learn more about God and maybe figure out what happened to me. I see now how pathetic of an attempt I made since I allowed other *priorities* to take precedence over my relationship with God. But, God was not willing to give up on me, and soon I would find *much* more free time on my hands.

Even though there was supposedly not much evidence against me, I was terrified. It seemed like nothing was going on, and my wife and I felt sure the government would see that I did not do anything intentionally wrong. However, my paid attorney was not doing as nearly as much as what I felt he should have done. His investigation did not seem to expand beyond asking me a mere thirty-to-forty minutes of "badgering" questions. He did not get the forensic PC expert like he said he would, and he did not get the forensic psychiatrist as he promised. Furthermore, he did not even use the PC expert I had found him for free. Granted, he did talk to the PC expert (who was my friend at the time), but for some reason he never used him.

Sentencing day finally arrived, and I was sure I was looking at probation, a fine, or both. However, the Assistant Defense Attorney decided to throw in a few things that were not signed by all parties in the plea agreement. (Apparently, a lot of federal prisoners have experienced this.) Furthermore, the pre-trial supervisor that interviewed me incorrectly said that I told him I had met with two *minor* girls when I actually told him I met five *women*. As a matter of fact, I was even wrong at the time. In actuality, I had met with four women, two of whom were twenty-one-years-old while the other two women were even older than me! Though it doesn't make it morally right, what I had done was not illegal because they were all of legal age.

It was also said that I took pictures of a minor girl in a hotel room years before. In response to that accusation, my wife put on her "P.I. cap" and did some investigating of her own. She found proof that the woman in question was not a minor. I already knew this since I had seen a copy of her driver's license at the time of the incident.

Since none of this information was part of the plea agreement, I was not charged with any of it, so there was no legal reason to bring it up. Well, because of the illegal content that I had blindly included in my trading files, I was charged with one count of interstate transportation of child pornography and sentenced to eighty-seven months in federal prison. The judge said he was giving me the low end of the sentencing bracket because of my attempt to rehabilitate myself: I had entered therapy before the end of the month that I was busted. I was taken out of the courtroom in handcuffs right then and there. My mother, sister, and brother were sitting in the courtroom in tears, but I was not permitted to say goodbye to them. I believe this was the epitome of cruelty and inhumanity not only to me, but to my family.

After sitting in lock-up in the courthouse for four-to-five hours I was placed in handcuffs and shackles, which were also tightened down with a waist chain. (I'll be honest: I think these cuffs and shackles were the most traumatic part of this whole experience.) I was taken to a federal detention center along with two other guys. These idiots were joking and laughing like this was a damned joy-ride!

When we arrived at the detention center, we had to go into a room with about forty other guys also waiting to be processed. We were stripped naked, given ill-fitting prison jumpers, and our personal clothes were sent home. My wife said she was hit hard when she received the box of clothes devoid of a note of any kind. It was kind of like putting another nail in the coffin.

During processing, the Federal Detention Center's medical/psychology staff decided to put me on suicide watch because when I was asked if I had any suicidal ideations, I answered them honestly: "Yes." Being placed on suicide watch was not fun, in *any* sense of the word. Have you heard the phrase "padded cell"? Well, they got 'em! After being held in the detention center for about seven weeks, I was transferred to my final destination. I still had no idea where it would be because I was never told. The information was supposedly kept from us for security reasons, but I think it was held back more for playing head games than anything else. On went the cuffs and shackles again.

Several of us were put on the bus. There were two officers sitting in the front, behind a fenced door with shot guns, and then one officer was in the back with a shot gun. One of the officers made a loud announcement, "I suggest that you all behave yourselves and not cause any trouble. It's simple. If we get into an accident…you all WILL die!" In other words, they could not let anyone escape, so they would have to shoot you. Who knows if they were serious or not, but the shot guns told me to behave myself and "play nice".

Our final destination was not where we ended up that day. We had a layover at a penitentiary. This place looked like it could be Dracula's castle or some sort of medieval castle. It was creepy and gloomy. We were unshackled and put in a holding cell, again with about forty other guys. We sat in there a good two to three hours on a cold concrete floor with one filthy toilet that had no privacy. We were once again stripped and forced to put on a different set of prison "jammies". Brown bagged sandwiches were then handed out because we hadn't eaten since much earlier that morning. Once we had been somewhat accounted for, we were led to medical services.

When I arrived at medical services, I was greeted (in a loose sense of the word) by a lady. She asked me the normal doctor-type of questions at first. Then, she got to the suicidal ideation question. I was really depressed that day, so when she asked me the question, I started tearing up, and I once again answered honestly, "Yes." She just stopped what she was doing, picked up the phone and simply said, "I have another one for you."

A few minutes later a lieutenant came in, looked at me and said, "Who wants to kill themselves?" I never had a chance to answer because the cold-hearted woman pointed to me and said, "Him." The lieutenant said to the nurse, "Give me the knife in your desk, I will show him how to do it properly!" He then took my bagged sandwich and threw it in the trash, saying that if I was going to kill myself, then I wouldn't need to eat.

After that, he roughly spun me around and threw cuffs on me. He walked me through the halls and up to the lieutenant's office where there happened to be about six to seven other officers. He led me to the middle of the room, where he removed the handcuffs and tried to instigate an argument with me. He attempted to provoke me into swinging at him. Now, as I saw it, if I had swung at him, as he outright suggested, the others, along with him, would have had the excuse to beat the hell out of me, or worse, shoot me. I wasn't falling for that.

Then, one punk who sat behind the desk asked me why I was there (believe it or not, it is illegal for them to ask). I told him the truth: one count of interstate transportation of child pornography. I foolishly tried to explain what had happened, but I was out of my element. These guys didn't want to hear anything in my defense. In their minds, as I found out later, if you have *anything* to do with kids, accidental or not, then you must have been physically molesting them too. I think they were probably bored and wanted some fun. I just happened to be their source for entertainment.

The officer behind the desk asked me, "You have kids, McDowell?" I told him, "Yes." He then proceeded to ask (and, I quote), "You F__k your kid?" Dear God, forgive me, but I really wanted to tell him, "No! Do you?!" Common sense said to keep my mouth shut, so I did. I was cuffed again and led into the basement where there was a four-by-five-by-six-foot cage. Yeah, a dog cage!

I was thrown in there and told to strip down because I didn't deserve clothes. I was left like that for an hour or so. I don't remember if I asked the officer if I could see the psychiatrist or if he asked me if I wanted to see the psych, but I can't really see them caring if I was depressed or not.

Anyway, they gave me a pair of boxers to put on because the psychiatrist was coming. She came in and asked her questions. I told her my side; about my mistakes and how nothing was intended to be illegal on my part, etc. She broke away to talk on the phone. Believe it or not, after all the horrors and depression I had been through, I was thinking to myself that this lady had a really nice looking behind. I was fantasizing even in this situation!

I was cuffed again and led into the hallway. The lieutenant said to me, "You pedophile, you're going to jail!" Well, I didn't think he was taking me to Taco Bell! What he didn't tell me was that I was not going where the others from the bus went. They went to general population. I was being led to where the "lifers" are locked up. You know, the ones that will *never* leave the jail. I did not have a good feeling about this. When we got to the entrance of that area, the lieutenant told me to stop. When I did he blurted out loudly, "BABY RAPER ON THE FLOOR!" I could hear the inmates jumping up to the doors with their faces pressed against the little narrow windows.

The lieutenant told me to move to the last cell at the end of the hall. I started walking and he told me to slow down. He was relishing in my terror. He told me to slow down even more, that there was no rush. Finally, he put me in the cell. It had a flat metal cot (like a mortician's autopsy slab). I just dropped and tried to sleep. Unfortunately, the inmate in the next room had other plans. He kept banging something on the wall, yelling how he was going to kill the "baby-raper", and that I'd have to go to the showers at some time. He must have kept that up for a good two hours, or so it seemed.

At about 5:00am I was awakened to be transported to my final destination. I thank God that I did not have to stay at this penitentiary for any longer than one night. I was told that it was highly unusual to be there for less than a week or two, sometimes even longer. I honestly did not think I was going to live long enough to leave this particular layover because all indications pointed towards me getting "shanked," which was very common in that place. Sadly, this was only a small part of what had actually happened.

I finally arrived at the federal prison where I would be held for the duration of my sentence. I sat and waited in the Special Housing Unit (SHU) (a.k.a. "segregation" or "the hole"). In this unit, they held those who were being disciplined, placed under investigation, or just waiting for a bed to open up in the housing units ("general population"). In SHU, the only entertainment was watching the dust float around and watching your hair grow. I'm not kidding. Unless you could get hold of a book, writing materials, or a radio, there was *nothing* to do. I sat in there for ten days. Not my choice for a vacation, believe me.

I eventually made it to my housing unit and was put in there with two other inmates. After getting somewhat used to the new living conditions, I found the chapel. The entire time I was in prison, the chapel was the only place where I felt comfortable. While in the chapel I met Dana, who played the organ (and any other instrument you could name) and sang during all of the Christian services. I found out that he ran a Bible Study Group in my living unit, and I jumped on the invitation to join. Being a part of this group helped to calm me down and make friends. Some of these friendships lasted the entire time I was locked-up.

Dana saw my sincere desire to learn more about God as well as to shed my sinful lifestyle. One day, he told me about "Christian Bible College and Seminary" (C.B.C.S.), which is a non-profit college that is geared towards God, not so much on profit. You can easily earn all four degrees—associate's, bachelor's, master's, and doctoral—for fewer than ten thousand dollars. It sounded good, especially since potential students are able to defer tuition until prison sentences are finished and a job is obtained. Furthermore, it's not a diploma mill; you have to do the work! This opportunity was a no-brainer. After receiving my wife's O.K., I registered for my associate's degree in Bible Studies 1.

I did not waste my time while in prison. I earned an associate's degree in Bible Studies 1, a bachelor's degree in Biblical Counseling, a master's degree in Christian Counseling, and started a doctoral degree in Christian Counseling, which I am currently completing. As I had mentioned earlier, since I did not find the time on my own to learn about God, He was clearly making it possible for me to learn about Him, in depth, with less distractions or worries of a home life. As time went on, being placed in prison was the best thing for me (even though I desperately wanted to go home) and, while in there, many doors were opened up to me that normally are not opened in the prison system.

Through all the stress, fear, frustration, and depression I had been experiencing, you would think that my less-than-religious-dreams and thought patterns would have at least been put on the back burner, temporarily. Nope! So, I asked about seeing a therapist. I was brushed aside time and again until one day I came across a posting on a bulletin board about a self-help group held in the psychology department. I immediately signed-up for it.

I was called to the psych department and was interviewed by "Dr. M." for the group. I opened right up about my charges. In response, the doctor told me that I might want to come up with a story to tell in the group. I said I would try to avoid direct answers, but I was not going to outright lie because it would get too complicated, and I didn't have the freedom to just get up and leave if I wanted to go. Therefore, I decided to stay "transparent" because if I lied, God could not bless my efforts. I decided to leave it in God's hands.

I attended a few of the sessions but was not able to really open up like I wanted. I did not know these people, and all but one of these guys were hardcore drug-dealers. The odd one was just in therapy for gambling in the units. This was not doing me any good. I went to "Dr. M." after one of the sessions and told him, but he did not want me to drop-out. I asked him if I couldn't talk about *my* addiction, how was I able to benefit from the therapy. He then offered to see me one-on-one if I stayed in the group because he saw my sincerity for rehabilitation and sobriety of my porn lifestyle. He went on to say that in his thirteen years of working for the Bureau of Prisons (BOP), one-on-one counseling sessions were highly unusual but that it would be made available for me if I wanted it. (Well, the BOP is regularly providing the sessions now because one-on-one counseling has proved to work out very well. They have even hired a few more therapists for this very purpose.)

Even with all this counseling, I felt most of my problems were spiritual in nature. "Dr. M." incorporated religion into our sessions, but his field was specified in psychology, not religion. He felt the need to ask "Chaplain H." to talk to me. This particular chaplain allowed God's word to be the final word, not the BOP's. His boss was God, and he did not hide that fact. Furthermore, he did not harass the inmates. He would rather hug the inmates and show the power of prayer. He was a true minister in every sense of the word. Between Dana, "Dr. M", and "Chaplain H.", I have no doubt that I was divinely led to this particular federal prison instead of one of the several that were closer to my home.

"Chaplain H." and I talked for a bit. I told him about my constantly immoral wandering mind and how the images disturbed me. I also mentioned how I felt that they were demonic in nature. He sympathized but claimed these behaviors did not seem like anything out of the ordinary. But when I mentioned that even during church service my mind wondered, like when I say the "Hail Mary" and Mary becomes part of my putrid thoughts. "Chaplain H." stopped dead in his tracks and called one of his friends. He told his friend, Lee, that he had a job that was out of his own league. This actually scared me. Did he think I was possessed or something?

Lee and a volunteer from "Prison Fellowship," Linda, were trained in Theophostic disciplines. The two evaluated me and learned of my septic-tank thought patterns and my anger issues. This six-week course went on for approximately ten weeks. I was pretty "wacked-out," and Lee thought I would be a good candidate for a course called "Falling Forward," a Christian course on sexual impurity that was supposed to take twenty-seven weeks to complete. However, it took us a year-and-a-half! I was badly off, but I did learn more about myself as well as what was going on in my heart and puny brain.

During the completion of the "Falling Forward" course, I read a chapter about once a week on my own. Every Thursday night, the three of us would get together to go over what I read and see what I had gotten out of the chapter. Then, we would apply it to my life. Linda and Lee would not stop until I understood what I read. They were very good about that. Together we would explore my feelings, my messed up emotions (which were really mixed-up), my warped thoughts and dreams. We found most were biblically found to be demonic in nature. This is *not* saying that I was possessed. Satan is very real, and most people are in some way "influenced" by his evil nature. I was just exceptionally influenced, mostly out of ignorance.

The other side of the coin is also true. Since Satan is real, then God is also very real. With Theophostic ministry, Lee and Linda showed me how to turn over my dreams for permanent disposal, which works kind of like a computer hard drive. In my mind, I envisioned Jesus taking each disturbing image from my hand as I handed them over to Him. He in turn would throw them into the Lake of Fire. Rarely did these particular images ever bother me again. Each time an image would enter my mind, I would go to prayer and hand over the image to Jesus to do what I cannot: rid myself of the image.

When questions came up that neither Lee or Linda could answer, they did not try to cover up the fact that they did not know. We would go into prayer and Lee would "talk" to Jesus. Lee is not a modern day prophet or anything, but prayer is nothing more than communication with God. What better way for us humans to communicate with our God than to talk to Him? Lee would open up in prayer and then ask Jesus questions. Lee never tried to assume that Jesus would answer him and thus manipulate any answers. Lee told me that Jesus would answer me, but only I would know in what form He would accomplish this. I came to understand when Jesus answered me, and I know Jesus loves me even after all these years of constant worshipping of porn.

Lee and Linda stuck with me until all the troubled areas were either fixed or I had the coping skills to work on them myself. They helped to reaffirm God's love for me, and because of this I was able to see that everything I had been through since 2001 had been prearranged by God to reclaim one of His children (remember the one lost sheep story?) and bring Himself glory, which is His due.

Through reflecting upon the events that transpired after I sought God's help, I see now that every step of my journey had a purpose for my healing. I had to hit rock bottom so Jesus could pick me up again. I had to experience the trials of court in order to see how wrong I had been with engaging in the evils of porn. I had to go through hell in the penitentiary, where I was degraded of my human form, so I could see what I *could* have had to deal with in serving out my sentence. But, instead, God placed me in a prison where I received *love* and *support* from individuals in a prison system that is virtually devoid of love and care. The Lord guided me to Dana, "Dr. M", "Chaplain H.", Lee and Linda, and others to help me flush away my messed up mind, and put on new eyes with the guidance of the Holy Spirit.

All of the people I encountered along my journey of healing in prison nurtured my studies, helped me to rebuild my self-esteem, and guided me back on the right path. God even helped me to learn about His nature and how to properly interpret His words, with supervision readily available. And through it all, God blessed me with the love and support of a caring family—I have seen how others in prison have completely lost the support and contact of their families. God covered all the bases. All I can say now is, glory and praise be to Jesus!

I close here by telling you that I would *never* have been able to regain control on my own. It took our Heavenly Father to show me how lost I was. It took our Heavenly Father's agape love to forgive my sins and allow me back into His family. It took our Heavenly Father to organize and *provide* the timing, people, and organizations it would take to change me as well as to help keep me in check. With all that I have learned, I pray that through our Father's will, I will be able to help others avoid what I have gone through. And, by the grace of God, I'll do it!

Jim McDowell

4

God is Healing

"The wound is the place where the Light enters you."

– Rumi

Mercy Heals

Ever since I can I remember I have had a rocky relationship with my sister-in-law, Jane. For reasons that are unbeknownst to me, Jane has never fully accepted me for who I am, portraying the notion that she rejected me as a valued individual long ago. Unsurprisingly, family gatherings were painful when we were both in attendance and I always felt so unwelcomed in her company.

Despite the little care Jane has shown towards me over the years, I have sought over and over again to no avail her approval. I was naively searching for something she was unable to give, yet since family has always been important to me, it was imperative that this relationship with my sister-in-law work. Unfortunately, this was nearly impossible since she seemingly wanted nothing to do with me. These discouraging feelings became rooted in my very being after constantly being exposed to one negative experience after another with her, ingraining them into my heart.

Well, there came a point when I felt like I was literally breaking down in the midst of this tremulous relationship. I remember one evening when I shut myself in the bathroom and cried to the Lord—asking Him, pleading with Him—to please give me some insight into why I struggle so much with this person. I wanted to understand how to deal with it in order to move forward and beyond the pain. That very night I woke up from sleeping and was graciously given clarity about the situation. God helped me understand why I feel and react the way I do around this person by sharing with me the following analogy:

You are like a deer in an open meadow. There is a hunter lurking close by. You have no idea where he is hiding, but he has a loaded gun. You are right in the middle of this meadow where there is nowhere to hide. Now, don't get shot.

But, God wanted me to trust in Him as my protector. Even though the hunter *will* find me, there *will* be a chase, and a bullet may graze me, He *will not* let that hunter take me down.

God knows that this particular relationship places me at a heightened anxiety. When it came to the "fight-or-flight" response of anxiety, I would fight. But, God wanted me to know that there was no need to fight—God was going to do that for me, but in His way. And He did. God really came through for me and in ways I could have never imagined…

A couple of months following this gift of insight, Jane came over to visit with my kids and I was having a hard time dealing with her presence in my house. So, I fought back by ignoring her. I firmly believe that Satan had seen this window of weakness within me and he pounced on it. I felt like I was being attacked on the inside: it was as though I was being constricted, as if someone was slowly, yet meticulously, squeezing me internally. The goodness of my heart was being suffocated and berated at the same time. These feelings darkened my thoughts and angered me. I withdrew from the company of my sister-in-law and busied myself with other tasks, ultimately retreating to the upstairs to have some time to myself. As I sat upstairs I could feel the attack on my thoughts and my heart strengthen—I was being bombarded with the remembrance of horrible things that had been said and done in the past by this person. It didn't matter if the hurt happened recently or long ago, the reminders of each incident were flooding my soul. My heart was being so hardened that I could barely squeeze out the few words to the Lord, "Help me. I cannot help myself." But, I did and that was enough. God heard my cry for help. He crumbled the wall that was building-up within me and softened my heart. Because of God's grace, I was freed from the onslaught of feelings that were darkening my soul, and the true character that God had molded for me over the years was brought to the forefront; He rescued me from the grips of my attacker. God gently gave me a push in the right direction and the Holy Spirit led the way for me, ultimately enabling me to have a pleasant time during the remainder of my sister's-in-law visit.

That evening, after Jane had left, my husband, children and I went to Mass. I was feeling so unworthy of being there in His church because of my weakness in the presence of my sister-in-law. I felt guilty for my inability to be the bigger person during encounters with her and not being able to exemplify the calling of a good Christian: to love others as Jesus loves us. God had taught me and shared with me so much over the years and even promised that He would take care of everything for me with regards to my sister-in-law, but I still doubted Him. And for that I felt so ashamed. Yet, God chose this time—the time of my feeling of complete unworthiness—to show His great love for me through the gift of mercy. And, He showed this love through my children.

All throughout Mass, my children hugged me, kissed me, modeled exceptional behavior, and were just overflowing with love towards me. It was so powerful that it was clear this love was coming from God. He spoke to my heart in ways only I would understand and the message He shared was filled with merciful love. During those precious moments, His mercy healed my wounded heart, rejuvenated my soul, and enflamed my desire to forgive Jane and encouraged me to let go of past hurts.

I now understand what it is like to be shown mercy—oh, what a beautiful feeling it invokes! God has shown me the healing power that comes from this precious gift. And, now God wants me to share that same mercy with the one who has hurt me the most. So, true to His promise to those who come to Him, He answered my cry for help when I asked God to show me how to move forward and beyond the pain. He replied, "Healing is found through mercy."

Anonymous

Hope

I was in an on-again-off-again relationship with a particular individual for a little over a decade. I met him when I was thirteen; we went to grade school together, and I had been involved with him ever since. What originally started as an innocent grade-school crush developed into something deeper—an attachment. What was once puppy love morphed into an unrequited love...on my end. There was lying, cheating, and just a general lack of trust and respect involved. I grew up in a stable and loving family, but I created for myself almost a second life. One that was full of insecurity, dependence, and looking back, emotional abuse. On one hand I was an upstanding, smart, and responsible teenager (and young adult) who excelled in school, but on the other—on the inside—I was emotionally crippled, insecure, and desperately trying to win the love and acceptance of a man whose love I could not gain.

Steven was the first boy I ever really cared about. I turned to him for emotional support; I confided in him. I believed we had a connection no one else could understand, so when the red flags of an unbalanced relationship began to surface, I ignored them. After grade school we went to different high schools, and later, different colleges. Over the years, I attempted to pursue other relationships, but Steven was always on the forefront of my mind and heart. He was my priority. I ignored the standards I expected from men and made exceptions to the moral principles I demanded others to uphold in relationships. I hardened my heart. I prayed for God to help me time and time and again, but I didn't have the will power to do what I knew I needed and should do: break things off with Steven. I cared about him too much. And, because I knew what I had with him was unhealthy—and thus, made me look pathetic—I didn't really share my ongoing relationship with him with anyone, at least not in detail. Twelve years later, among one of my many desperate attempts to make this man love me, I became pregnant. I was twenty-five-years-old.

I experienced a lot of emotions when I first found out I was pregnant. First, I was in a state of disbelief: I couldn't believe it, there was no way I could actually be pregnant. Then, I was angry. I was angry with Steven; I was angry with myself. I was embarrassed—I couldn't believe I was that "girl"! I never thought I would be *that* girl. Steven made it absolutely clear to me that he did not want a child. He was *not* going to have one. He didn't want to be with me, and he didn't want to be forced to be with me. He wanted me to have an abortion and forget anything ever happened. He told me he'd go with me to a clinic. He'd even go with me to confession afterward… and then we could stay friends. In his mind, it was just that simple. However, for me, abortion was not an option. It never was and it never would be. This disconnect was, from his point of view, a betrayal. So, I was on my own.

I remember seeing her for the first time with the ultrasound. I stared at that little shrimp-like creature in the picture and listened to her heart beat. I couldn't believe I was looking at a tiny human being—a baby… *my* baby. A baby created with a man I loved and wanted so much to be with despite my better judgment. I fell in love with her. However, adoption was one of the first words out of my mouth when I shared with my family I was pregnant. It was a protective reflex I blurted out for fear I would be judged. I wanted a family, I still do, but I wasn't ready to be a single mother who would be solely responsible for my child. I wanted to raise her with my husband, but I did not have one. I wanted to be present while she grew up and not have to pawn her off to the local daycare provider while I worked to support her (Steven made it clear that he would pay only what he was legally required, but even then he claimed he would make his money in ways that I would not be able to touch it). I could only imagine the nightmare of a battle I would have with him—in the courtroom and out. I didn't want that for my daughter. I wanted her to experience complete and unconditional love…from both of her parents. I asked Steven if he would give up his parental rights—maybe that would prevent her from experiencing the rejection I had experienced from him for years. Maybe if he was completely out of the picture—legally and physically, she wouldn't feel abandoned. He said no. I didn't ask again.

During my pregnancy, I experienced an amazing amount of love and support from people I never expected. However, there were also relationships that were tested and friendships that were broken for reasons I never could have predicted. My relationship with my sister was seriously tested—to a point where I didn't think we'd ever speak again (we had always been pretty close), and I was deeply hurt by some of the words and statements made by some of my loved ones—people from whom I wanted and expected unconditional love. My confidence in myself plummeted. Yet, my focus was not myself; it was her. My focus was Hope.

I cut off most contact with Hope's father, knowing the toxic relationship could affect her, even in utero. I ate healthily, exercised, and talked to her. I prayed with her. I played music for her. Told her how excited I was to meet her. I tried shielding her from the negative feelings that sporadically assaulted my heart because I didn't want her to be affected by them. I specifically remember driving home from work one day when a wave of despair washed over me. I turned on some music—the angriest music I could find. I let the notes play out my pain adjusting the volume the loudest it could possibly go. Then I turned it off. I didn't want Hope to feel the angry music, to feel the hurt I was feeling. I wanted her to feel safe and loved. I wanted her to know that despite everything she was loved. I started painting again. As corny as it sounds, painting became my prayer. I prayed continuously for guidance. For forgiveness. I prayed for God to take the pain of rejection from me, to help me make the best decision for Hope, to help me let go and give this situation to Him. I prayed for peace.

I remember calling Catholic Charities early in my pregnancy. I didn't know what I was going to ask or what I was going to say. All I ended up being able to do was cry. I felt foolish. I looked up information on adoption and birth mothers and I was disgusted with what I found. There were stereotypes and circumstances I didn't fit, nor did I want to. Here I was, a financially stable and educated young professional—I was not a kid. I was not promiscuous. I was not the considered "typical" birth mother. I even hated the term. I was not like "them". The research made me sick enough to abandon the idea of adoption altogether. However, I knew in my heart great things were in store for my daughter. If I could be strong enough for her now, somehow, at some point, we both would be rewarded. It was not until I was seven months pregnant that I called Catholic Charities again, and this time I scheduled an appointment. I trusted the Lord would guide me to either stop or continue with the process; and, I would be responsive to whatever it was He presented. I was amazed by what happened. I found a family—a family that met all the very specific criteria I required for my daughter. I was able to bypass the established protocol of placing my baby in foster care for the interim grace period (I was completely against placing Hope in foster care; she needed to be with her mother from the day she was born. I would not accept anything less for her). And, most importantly, I found peace in my decision. A peace that remained with me through the hell that was to follow.

My daughter was born in the early hours of a crisp fall morning. She was beautiful; I fell in love with her all over again. She had a full head of dark hair and the sweetest face I have ever laid eyes on. At 6 lbs. 11 oz., she was tiny. I couldn't stop looking at her. My mom and my sister were with me, along with two of my closest friends. Everyone was in tears. I was so happy.

I slept very little during my time in the hospital. I wanted to spend every second with Hope, my little girl. I nursed her and changed her diapers. When she cried, I would sing. I sang "Twinkle Twinkle Little Star" and Bob Marley's "Everything's Gonna Be Alright". I called Steven, and for the first time in nine months, I heard tenderness in his voice. I asked him if he'd like a picture of her and he said yes. I asked him if he would come see us. He said no. My heart sank. I kept waiting for someone to say something. I wanted someone to tell me to forget the adoption, forget the circumstances, and keep her. I wanted to keep her. I loved her.

I knew I could have changed my mind at any point. I knew I was not obligated to follow-through with adoption. I was her mother and I could raise her and she'd be fine. I could make things work. But that voice. That little voice in my heart—the one with so much wisdom and so much strength—I couldn't ignore it. It told me to let go. It was okay to let go. So, amidst the war of emotions and doubt, I trusted that voice, and I did. I let go.

Looking back, I cannot say how I did what I did. I don't know how at the end of the two-day hospital stay I was able to walk down the hospital corridor, place Hope in the bassinet, say a measly "I love you", and walk away. I don't know how I climbed into the back of my parents' car and rode all the way back to my parents' house, or what I was thinking when I walked aimlessly around the house not knowing what to do with myself. I felt nothing. I was numb.

Then it hit me.

I have never in my life felt so much anguish. I have never cried so hard. It was awful. It was painful. It was hell.

I couldn't sleep that night. I tossed and turned for hours, wrestling with grief and the withdrawal from my baby. I told myself that I would fix everything in the morning. I would not go through with the adoption, and I'd get her back tomorrow. With that, I was able to fall asleep.

But, I didn't terminate the adoption the next day. Or the day after that. I had Hope brought to me a couple of times over the course of the next few weeks before I even signed the adoption papers. One particular day, I was sitting on my parents' front porch swing with Hope, bundled tightly, sleeping peacefully in my arms. She looked so sweet. I looked out across the porch and saw an image of her playing in the front yard with her daddy—a daddy I couldn't offer her, at least not now. Both of them were laughing. She was happy. She was so happy… I called the case worker and told her I was ready to sign the adoption papers.

Even after signing the adoption papers, I had a thirty-day "grace" period to change my mind. I wrestled with it. I wrestled with Steven. I wrestled with God. I begged Him for clarity. He told me to trust in Him. I didn't know what that meant. Was I doing the right thing? I picked up the phone a few times to stop the process, but I never went through with the call. For the last week of the grace period—before the adoption became legal and finalized—I flew out to the other side of the country to give myself physical distance to prevent myself from making last minute drastic decisions. I was with some of my family, and I had all the love and support I could possibly need or want; yet, I felt so empty.

When day thirty came around, the last day of my grace period, I shared with some of my family members that I was having second thoughts. They jumped on it. One cousin was ready to buy a plane ticket for a red-eye back to my home state. Another promised to pay for a lawyer to address any legal issues that may arise and offered a room in her home with a live-in nanny for Hope and me. She assured me we could stay as long as I wanted—or until I could figure out my work situation and establish myself as a single mother. Still another cousin had been collecting clothes and small items I may need…just in case I changed my mind. I was offered everything I could possibly want and need. I had the support, I had the means, and I had even typed-up the text message to inform my case worker that I was not going to go through with the adoption.

But I couldn't press send.

There was so much going on in my head and heart. So much turmoil. Yet, amongst all the bewilderment remained a small steady feeling. It was constant and it was sure. It was the peace I had been praying for. It was the peace in knowing that despite the onslaught of emotions, I did not and would not regret the decision to love my daughter and offer her to a family that would also love her. It was a knowing, an acknowledgement, that by offering her to this family I was not any less of a mother or a person. I was not relinquishing my importance in her life or hers in mine; she was my daughter—she would always be my daughter. It was an assurance that what I was doing may hurt now, but I would not hurt forever; and, in the end, it would all be worth it. It was a promise that everything was going to be okay.

So, I deleted the text message, called my mom and unloaded the burden of my pain by yelling at her.

Hope is God's gift to me and to her adoptive family, and, I believe, a gift for Steven, too. Through her I was able to know love. I was able to break the chain that bound me to Steven, yet gifted a link to the very best of him—the best of him that is in her. What I couldn't do for myself I could do for her, which then empowered me to do what was necessary for me. Having her and being her mother changed my life. Going through with the adoption wasn't easy and it still isn't. There was nothing graceful about the way I handled anything, and there are still periods of heartache—but it's bearable.

My experience with Hope helped melt my half-frozen heart and open my eyes to see that I had spent almost half of my lifetime building barriers between me and others. I didn't realize how guarded I was, how much hurt I inflicted on others in effort to prevent any more damage done to me, or how raw and deep the scars of my relationship with Steven actually ran. Layer by layer, those walls are crumbling, exposing me to an even greater gift: the gift of vulnerability; the gift of love; and, the ultimate gift of dependence, complete trust, and a closer relationship with our Lord. My journey—emotional and spiritual—is far from over. I'm still learning to accept and love myself. I'm still learning to let others love me—that it's even possible for someone to love me. I'm healing. And so far, it has all been worth it.

Anonymous

The Road Less Traveled

Growing up, my family and I attended a traditional Catholic church. I am the youngest of three children and all three of us hated going to church on Sunday mornings. The sermons were lost on us. My mom hoped attending would help give us structure and build moral judgment, but looking back I don't think she actually believed much of what was taught.

My mother and father lived separate lives prior to their physical separation. My father has always been atheist and did not attend church with the family despite my mom's urging. The year I turned seven my grandfather passed away from lung cancer, and I think my mom began seriously questioning her faith or lack thereof. My mom watched Grandpop slowly deteriorate over months until he finally passed on. She said he was nothing more than skin and bones, and that she wished it wasn't the last image she had of her father. Mom always doubted God's presence in her life and I guess Grandpop's death confirmed her doubt. She pulled my siblings and me out of church for good.

Over the years God and religion fell to the back of my mind. I found that I would only call on God when times were tough. I'd ask Him "why me?" I blamed Him and I questioned His existence. I'd retained nothing from the brief time I had attended church. I questioned the point of life, what my purpose was on this planet, and I was consumed by negative thoughts. In middle school I developed social anxiety and depression… something I still struggle with today. My parents never had a loving relationship, it was strictly business. My father grew distant and apathetic; my mother was filled with resentment. I knew my parents loved me, but in a way I felt abandoned by them. They separated when I was sixteen, and this terrible void grew in my heart. Life was turning out to be very different from what I thought it should be.

I started looking for love in all the wrong places. I wanted so desperately to be loved and protected and to feel like I belonged. I drank until I blacked out nearly every weekend, and I was promiscuous. After many failed relationships—unhealthy abusive relationships—I began to realize that I was looking for something bigger in my life…something deeper, but what?

I eventually found myself in the most poisonous relationship I've ever been involved with. He made me believe that I was the love of his life, only to find out that he had been lying and cheating on me almost the entire time we were together. I ended it, but I was left broken and feeling really hopeless about love and life.

I began seeing a therapist. I didn't know who to turn to for help, and needed some objective advice. During those sessions I played with the idea of attending a local church. It was something that just sort of popped in my head as a healthy alternative to my constant self-medicating. It took many more months for me to actually seek out a church. During that time, I sought guidance from friends and family and wasn't making much progress. I was taking antidepressant medication...wasn't really getting anywhere...I just felt so empty inside. So one day I hopped on Google and searched for local churches. I found one and really liked its message of "Church for people who don't go to church". The first service I attended centered on forgiving others and mending broken relationships. I felt something stir in the hollow space inside of me during worship. It brought me to tears. I felt like I was finally home and that I was deeply loved...I realized I had been the whole time. For the first time in my life I felt God's endless love and forgiveness for me.

In the short time that I have found my faith, I've learned that my suffering has helped me grow and it has brought me closer to God than I ever thought possible. It took me exhausting all other avenues and hitting rock bottom to seek Him out. I often wonder when or if I would have found Him otherwise, and I'm so grateful I have. Nothing I went through was in vain because it brought me to Jesus. I see the beauty all around me and thank God every day for curing me of my blindness. I know the sacrifices Jesus made for us and that nothing He asks of us is too much. It's kind of ironic that bad experiences with the wrong people ultimately helped me find my faith in God, and now God is helping me rebuild my faith in man.

B. Davila

Believing is Seeing

"Because he clings to me I will deliver him; because he knows my name I will set him on high. He will call upon me and I will answer; I will be with him in distress; I will deliver him and give him honor. With length of days I will satisfy him, and fill him with my saving power." (Psalm 91:14-16 NABRE)

This passage reminds me how the magnificent, wonderful, and awesome God has worked through my life. I am an educator. I worked at St. John's Institute, a Catholic and Chinese institution in Bacolod City, Negros Occidental Philippines. I was teaching Computer and Science to the students of the second, fourth and sixth grades in the elementary department.

On May 14, 2010, the school administrators sent a group of us teachers to Manila, Philippines to attend a one-week seminar for computer teachers. After arriving in the Manila airport, our supervisor from CAL (Computer Assisted Learning) brought us to the hotel so we could drop-off our luggage in our rooms and freshen-up before we went to Mass.

After attending Mass, my co-teachers and I were exiting the church when I accidentally stumbled. My vision became distorted after I fell: I was seeing double. It was hard for me to look at my surroundings because of the distortion. I felt dizzy, nauseas, and had a constant headache. Later that morning, I was rushed to the hospital, completely unaware that what I was experiencing is commonly the first sign of a brain stem stroke or diplopia. Diplopia is a pathological condition of vision in which a single object appears double, more commonly known as double vision.

Once I was checked into the Eye Center of Medical City, the nearest hospital to our hotel, I was seen by an ophthalmologist. Oddly enough, there were no problems found with my eyes, so I was advised to undergo a CT scan. Because the double vision persisted, I sought a second opinion from another doctor because I was in doubt with the results of the first exam. So, I went to see a neurologist to check my eyes and brain and was admitted at World City Medical Center. After examining my eyes and brain, the neurologist recommended that I receive a CT scan, but ironically the hospital's CT scan-machine was defective. I signed a waiver and was discharged from the hospital, resigned to the fact that there was nothing more to be done to address my double vision while I was in Manila. I had no choice but to wait for my scheduled flight to Bacolod, Philippines, where I would then visit Riverside Hospital and have my CT scan done. Thankfully, Mr. and Mrs. Lizares, parents of two of my students, were kind enough to help me find a good neurologist back home.

When I arrived at Riverside Hospital in Bacolod, I had a consultation with the neurologist Dr. Michelli Yusay. Following my examination, Dr. Yusay formed the following impressions: severe migraine, brain stem stroke, and aneurysm. Mind you, these were merely her impressions, not an actual diagnosis. I then had a CT scan, which showed a normal impression and that there was nothing wrong that could be found. Dr. Yusay suggested I go for another test, a MRA (Magnetic Resonance Angiography)—a type of MRI that focuses on blood vessels instead of brain tissue—that can detect the inner portion of the brain. She wanted to make sure all the veins were normal and that there was no clot or abnormal growth present that could lead to an aneurism.

At this point in time, I was unable to utilize any insurance benefits through work and was solely responsible for paying my medical expenses. The MRA suggested by Dr. Yusay would entail a huge cost, which troubled me because I could not financially afford the anticipated amount. Furthermore, as the provider of my family's main source of income, I had to make sure I could continue to work. To ease the difficulty of the situation, I was blessed, by God's grace, with help from the generous administrators and moral support of those who surrounded me: the school director, Msgr. Noly Que, LRMS; the school principal, Fr. Garry Neil Fuentebella, LRMS; my mother, Ma Fe De Jesus; my spiritual advisor, Ruby Saril; the school nurse; my fellow teachers; and some generous parents from the school.

With financial help from the aforementioned people, I underwent an MRA, MRI and all the lab tests suggested by Dr. Yusay. All the tests revealed normal findings. There were eight to ten expert doctors examining me and consulting on my situation. They had a difficult time understanding my sudden illness and determining my condition. It was a rare kind of disease. They went on to inform me that it would likely take years (although they were unsure about how many years) before I could see normally again. The lack of information that the doctors provided took a mental toll on me, and I cried every night. I was stressed, anxious, paranoid, and dangerously lingering on the edge of depression. I felt completely useless.

Though I was struggling, I didn't give up. Instead, I found myself praying the Rosary every day, sometimes twice a day. I used to put the rosary beads on my eyes, head, and neck after I finished praying it. Not able to rely on the doctors and medicine to heal me, I looked to the Rosary as my medicine. In my prayer, I always reflected upon these words that were inspired by the Roman officer seeking Jesus' healing of his servant in Matthew 8:5-13: "Lord, I am not worthy to receive you, but only say the word and I shall be healed."

In addition to incorporating prayer into my daily routine as a way to help alleviate my anxiety over the situation, I continued to teach at St. John's Institute, despite my difficulty with seeing. It was very hard for me to prepare the lesson plans, create the visual aids, and present the lessons; but the thought of helping my students learn motivated me to keep going. I was so happy to share with them how God was working through my life. In that way, I inspired them. In turn, they were very participative and energetic every time I entered their classroom, and I found that they looked forward to my presence. The connection I felt with the students and their excitement to learn made all the long hours that I put into each lesson plan worthwhile. They even called me Ms. Pirate because I had to wear an eye patch to assist in my visual therapy. Their light-hearted approach to the matter made me laugh and helped make the use of the eye patch less awkward.

I continued to keep holding onto Jesus to help me through each day. I always offered my day to Him, telling Him to take charge in my place in case I lost strength. Being a living testimony of faith, hope and love is an awesome thing to give glory to God.

As a result of my dedication with work, I received the Early Bird Award and perfect attendance. The obstacles I faced on a daily basis with teaching and my double vision inspired my students, co-teachers, school personnel, and even my students' parents. I felt so blessed because even though I had a cross to bear, God sent angels to help me carry it. Those angels were my mom and dad, my sisters, my brother, my family, my close friends, school administrators, the school nurse, co-teachers who were there for me through thick and thin, and some of the parents who gave me financial support.

Then, on October 3, 2010, I woke up on my birthday with the ability to see normally. The double vision had disappeared. Though the doctors believed it would take years for my vision to return to normal, God gifted me with the beauty of sight within *six months* of the onset of my double vision. What a blessed birthday from Almighty God!

God's steadfast presence in my life is why I never gave up hope, and I attribute my quick recovery to the power of faith. God is really Awesome. And today as I write this, I am enjoying my new life with my husband, Robert, and our children, Theoden Skyler and Tia-Brielle, in the United States of America. It was through the belief in God and Jesus Christ that I am able to be here today to share this story with you and leave this legacy for my children and, God willing, my future grandchildren.

God has rewarded me greatly through my constant faith in Him, so I would like to end my story with this passage I live by: "Jesus told him, 'Have sight: your faith has saved you.' He immediately received his sight and followed him, giving glory to God. When they saw this, all the people gave praise to God" (Luke 18:42-43 NABRE).

Rowena De Jesus Villnave

When Life Shatters

Sometimes life shatters into a million, billion, zillion pieces. The rubble is left laying at our feet. There are big jagged shards that cut deep and leave scars, long and puckered. Then there are the little slivers that find their way under the skin and light a fire of pain that burns deep into the soul.

Yes, sometimes life shatters, and it happens to both believers and nonbelievers alike. No one is exempt. Suffering comes to us all.

What, then, are we to do?

Trust in God. The answer is easy, right?

So what's the hard answer, the one we turn to when all the scriptures we've learned have a hollow echo and when the drumbeat of our heart drowns out the words of God's ever faithful love? What do we do when trust is hard to come by and our faith feels, at best, distant?

Well, I know a thing or two about life shattering and can offer my sentiments to that question.

My daughter, Molly, wasn't quite two months past her ninth birthday when she began complaining of a headache. She wasn't one to normally complain, but this was the third time in the last four or five months that she'd had a headache. A visit to the ophthalmologist was in order, so it seemed. The cause of her headaches had to be simple. Molly was the only one in the family not yet wearing eyeglasses, and she finally needed them. After all, what else could it be? The pain got so bad, though, that she started crying, then vomiting, and I knew an eye exam wasn't going to fix the problem. We rushed her to the emergency room where a CT scan showed a tumor lodged deep in the occipital lobe of her brain.

She sobbed as they took her in for surgery. She pleaded with me to take her home. The headache was all gone, she said. She was fine—could we please leave the hospital? As a mom, I was used to comforting my children and soothing their fears. Even a mom's comfort, though, can only go so far when a surgeon tells your nine-year-old daughter the he's going to be operating on her brain. I could taste her terror, thick and acrid, and I cried out to God. There was no song I could sing or foul-smelling ointment I could apply to fix this for her. All I could do was pray… and trust.

Over eight hours later, I got to see my daughter again. It was late at night, and she was sedated, but she was breathtakingly beautiful. Over the coming days, they removed the breathing tube and the nasogastric feeding tube. She was eating solids, drinking her fluids, talking up a storm, and working hard in therapy. I watched my daughter relearn how to walk in a matter of days. She needed a walker and concentration, but she was amazing.

Then the surgeon told us his earlier fears were confirmed. He hadn't gotten the entire tumor. There would have to be a second surgery. I was disheartened, but I tried to keep it positive. She began recovering so quickly after the first surgery—the second one would be old hat, I reassured her. She'd know what to expect, and now she knew there was no need to be frightened. That's when she started to decline. Molly became less talkative and more resistant to taking her medicine. We all saw the change in her, and we thought she was upset about a second surgery. I couldn't blame her for that. I was upset too. As far as I was concerned, the sooner that second surgery came and went, the better. Then we could really get on that flower-strewn road to recovery.

A fever spike on the morning of the second surgery derailed our plans. Instead of going in to remove the remainder of the occipital tumor, the surgeon decided to insert an external ventricular drain (EVD) into the right lateral ventricle. The brain has four interconnected ventricles where its cerebrospinal fluid (CSF) is produced and circulated. Using an EVD to "tap into" one of the ventricles would allow the hospital staff to take samples of my daughter's CSF. Those samples, taken regularly over the next several days, were each cultured to look for any sign of infection. After all, fever usually means infection, and infection in the brain is a dangerous beast. Antibiotics used for treatment are carried by the blood to the affected part of the body. The brain, however, has a unique mechanism referred to as the blood-brain barrier. This barrier inhibits the blood's ability to safely deliver certain medications—including most antibiotics—to the brain.

One of the early cultures showed evidence of infection, but all the following cultures were clean. The specialists from Infectious Diseases put Molly on antibiotics to be on the safe side, but it was assumed the early culture had somehow been contaminated. Daily samples continued to be taken and cultured. Honestly, though, that seemed like the least of our problems at the time. Even though the procedure to insert the EVD hadn't been nearly as invasive as the first surgery, my daughter didn't awake from anesthesia as quickly as expected. Over a week went by, and she was still on a respirator. She was nonresponsive to personnel and barely responsive to her family. If I told her to squeeze my hand, she would—sometimes, but she had still not opened her eyes.

After the first surgery, Molly experienced nightmares. She would wake up during the night, screaming and begging me to protect Mango, her stuffed monkey and most prized possession. People were trying to drill a hole in Mango's head, she'd sob. She would plead with me to hide him, protect him, take him away. She wanted to shelter him, to keep him safe.

After the second procedure, I was the one having nightmares.

I'd sit there in Molly's room staring at the monitors, terrified to sleep because I was afraid she'd be gone by morning. I'd lay down and close my eyes only after I'd catch myself falling out of the chair because I'd nodded off. I slept with my glasses on so that when her monitor alarmed— which it did often because of how erratic her vital signs had become—I'd immediately be able to see what was wrong and not waste the three seconds it would take to put my glasses back on.

When I would finally allow myself to sleep, I'd wake up silently screaming. I couldn't remember the nightmares' details upon waking, but I always knew. The fear they left me with became a real thing with shape and form, and it stole my breath while it choked me. Sleep was not my friend. Awake, I could consciously choose to trust God with my daughter's life. Asleep, I lived every worst-case-scenario as I walked a tightrope across the bottomless gorge of doubt and helpless despair.

Then one morning a nurse was cleaning the mostly-healed surgical site at the back of Molly's head and puss came out. In a hospital where the average MRI wait seemed to be measured in terms of shifts rather than hours, getting an MRI that afternoon should have felt like a miracle. The news we received obliterated any positivity we'd tried to muster, though. Not only did Molly have an infection in her brain despite all the clean cultures and antibiotics, but that infection had caused a total of six separate strokes. No wonder she wasn't responding to us. She *couldn't* respond.

More surgery. Stronger antibiotics. Improvement.

Molly began responding to physical therapy once again. She couldn't sit up on her own, but when the therapist would pick up her foot and tell her to push, she would give it all she had. Little by little, she got better. We began hearing words like *residential rehab*. The future was far from certain—there was no way to know yet the extent of the damage from those strokes—but Molly was fighting, and we were right there with her fighting for her with everything we had.

Then she took a turn for the worse. She stopped responding. There was a rash, blood in her urine, and more. It was a classic allergic reaction to antibiotics. She'd already been on those antibiotics for a long time, but she seemed to have developed sensitivity to them. So we switched to a new antibiotic. Molly started to do better, then another reaction occurred. Then another. Stronger and stronger antibiotics were put into play with daily tests to watch liver function and other markers of toxicity.

Finally, at long last, the Infectious Diseases specialists determined that Molly was in the clear. They stopped the antibiotics. All the cultures were clean. Everything was looking up. Physical therapy was going so well that I'd toured the residential facility we hoped to get her into. It was three hours away, but there was a place that I could stay, too. The change would be positive. By then, Molly was strong enough to sit up. She needed pillows to help her stay in position, but her strength was coming back, and each day she responded better and better to therapy. She wasn't talking yet, but her attitude seemed positive.

The neurosurgeon wanted to do one last MRI before signing off on her release. We were scheduled for transport to the rehab center on a Monday, I think. That last MRI came right before the weekend. But it wasn't clean. There was a bright spot on the film, and bright spots mean infection.

More surgery.

We'd been in the hospital almost three months at that point. "The year she was nine," I would tell people, "won't be more than a blip on the radar when she's celebrating her ninetieth birthday with her family all around her." With each new trauma, though, being positive became harder.

Then we got good news. The bright spot wasn't infection after all. It was a small blood clot. Her doctors put in a subdural drain to be on the safe side. Our release to rehab would be delayed but not derailed. But, again, Molly didn't come out of anesthesia so well after that surgery. Rehab slowly slipped through our fingers, and we eventually discovered that she had contracted another infection in her brain.

The specialists from Infectious Diseases came up with a new antibiotic schedule, but Molly didn't respond any better this time than she had the last. She began reacting to other things—not just the antibiotics. At one point she went into anaphylactic shock following a treatment with albumin. Albumin is a protein she'd been given before with no problem. This time, as soon as the IV drip was started, her face and throat became alarmingly swollen. Had she not already been in a hospital where she could receive immediate treatment, she likely wouldn't have survived. Following that episode, she was on a steady drip of epinephrine—the medication from which the EpiPen gets its name. An allergist was called in to consult. After having never experienced an allergic reaction in her life, it didn't make sense that Molly was so suddenly allergic to everything.

As it turns out, the allergist who examined Molly was an immunoallergist—someone who specializes in both allergies and immunodeficiencies. He ran some extra tests because Molly's biological behavior was so unusual, tests a straight allergist wouldn't have thought to run. The results took days to come in. When they did finally come in, nobody understood them.

What chemo drugs had Molly been given? None, she was never on chemo. We were told she wouldn't need it. *Are you sure she was never on chemo?* Positive. Why? What's going on?

Molly, whose only significant illness up to that point in her life had been an umbilical hernia that was surgically treated when she was two, had SCID—a Severe Combined Immunodeficiency. My little girl, who had been the picture of health prior to the headache that prompted a trip to the ER, had a condition that should have ended her life years before. Children with SCID don't live the life my daughter had lived. They don't go to school, get colds, get their vaccines, and have surgery without anybody knowing they're ill. Children with SCID spend their entire all-too-brief childhoods in the hospital with infection after infection until somebody diagnoses the root problem. Undiagnosed, children with SCID rarely live to see their second birthday. So how could my daughter possibly have this debilitating illness without having had any symptoms until now? Nobody had answers, and more tests were ordered.

Then Molly started throwing up. A lot. Nearly twenty times in one night. And she began blistering all over her body: massive blisters, some of which were six inches long and stood nearly an inch off her skin, filled with fluid. Nobody could touch her without a blister bursting. She lost all her fingernails and toenails because blisters came up under them and forced them off.

A dermatologist was consulted, and a punch biopsy of her skin ordered. The biopsy results, however, proved inconclusive, telling us she either had toxic epidermal necrolysis (TEN) or graft versus host disease (GVHD). With the vomiting as a precursor to the blisters, the popular conclusion became GVHD. Molly had received blood more than once via transfusion since being in the hospital, but the blood she received was never irradiated. Why would it be? Only people with a recorded immunodeficiency receive irradiated blood.

Everybody's blood has different types of cells in it, and each of those cells performs its own function. The job of the white blood cell is to attack invading bodies and fight off infection. The process of irradiation kills the white cells in the new blood for one very important reason. If a person without their own immune system receives a transfusion of blood that hasn't been irradiated, the white blood cells in that transfused blood will see the person's entire body as an invading infection and will attack it. Because the person has no immune system, they can't fight off the attack, and GVHD is the result. With no history of immunodeficiency anywhere in Molly's medical history, there hadn't been any reason for her blood to be irradiated. Except that at some point and against all the odds, she developed SCID. As a result, the white blood cells in the blood she received attacked her body, leading to a horrifying case of GVHD.

There were days when I stood precariously on an ice-slicked slope, and at the bottom were anger, hopelessness, and bitterness. In a word, despair. I put spikes in the bottoms of my shoes and dug in, though, because my daughter needed me. She was depending on me to be strong for her, and I refused to lose my footing. Pure stubbornness fueled by the prayers of hundreds and the strength of God kept me from an emotionally and spiritually debilitating fall.

After she recovered from the GVHD, the next step was to internalize the EVD. Along the way, we discovered that her first through third ventricles had been cut off from her fourth ventricle. Whether because of scar tissue or some other unknown cause, the CSF her body was creating in those higher ventricles could not drain down to the fourth ventricle and into her spinal column the way it was supposed to. By then she was on what was probably her eighth EVD, but that couldn't be a permanent solution. They needed to move her from the external drain to a peritoneal shunt. The shunt, installed in the brain, would relieve pressure by allowing excess CSF to drain harmlessly into Molly's abdominal cavity rather than build up within her brain and cause further damage.

The internalization led to more complications. Protein in her CSF kept clotting within the shunt mechanism, making it useless. Without a way for her CSF to drain, it would just keep building up in her brain until it caused a catastrophic failure. Nothing more could be done.

Five months after Molly entered the hospital, we were finally allowed to take her home. She was no longer on a respirator by then, but she had a tracheostomy and a gastric feeding tube. She'd also suffered two more strokes. It had been about three months since she'd last shown signs of consciousness. Her eyes hadn't voluntarily opened since the surgery prompted by the bright spot on the MRI...mere days before we were supposed to have gone to rehab.

I asked one of the doctors what I was supposed to tell others. People would have questions about her condition, and I knew they wouldn't understand all the big medical terms I'd been forced to learn. "Tell them she's in a coma," she said with sad eyes. "That's a word they'll know."

We left the hospital filled with prayers for healing and recovery but knowing that, unless God intervened, we were taking her home to die. We never stopped believing that God could move mountains, nor did we stop asking Him to move one on our daughter's behalf. With each passing day we renewed our petitions for her life. As long as there was breath in her body, there was hope.

Molly stabilized almost as soon as we brought her home. Some of the issues she'd had toward the end of her hospital-stay dissipated. Nurses filled our home for part of each day, but we were together again as a family. We ate our meals together—though hers was through a feeding tube. We watched movies that had been Molly's favorite before she went into the hospital, laughing at all the funny parts, even if it was forced. "Remember that scene, Molly? When so-and-so did such-and-such? It's your favorite scene."

Meanwhile, the CSF continued to build up in her brain, and one day it was finally too much. Her brain stem could no longer process the signals that said her body had too much carbon dioxide and not enough oxygen in it, and so it stopped sending out the message that told her to breathe. And then there was no more breath in her body and no more hope.

She slipped away from us almost six months to the day after she'd begged me to take her home from the hospital. Her dad was on one side of her bed, and I was on the other. We each held a hand and told her over and over again how much we loved her, how amazing she was, and how blessed we were that she was our daughter. No matter how many times I've tried to write about that moment, to find the words to express the tangled knot of emotions I experienced, I fall short. The words may be out there, but I have yet to find them.

The day my daughter gained heaven is the day my life shattered in a million billion zillion pieces. That slope of ice under my feet gave way, and I fell into the midst of the scattered shards of everything my life—my daughter's life—was supposed to have been. My dreams, hopes, and heart were all broken that day. What on earth was I to do with all the fragmented pieces?

I believe that knowing the Bible is good but knowing how to *use* what it says is vital. Following my daughter's death, I learned some hard lessons about real-life application, not just of scripture, but of my faith, too. Those lessons didn't come easy.

Often, our first instinct when something breaks is to pick up the cracked and broken remains and see if we can put them back together. Whether a dinner plate or an antique vase, we will hold the fragments this way and that as we determine if there's any hope for resurrecting the broken piece. Life is no different. When our lives shatter, we stoop down and sweep the debris close to us so we don't lose anything. We look at the tangled mess from various angles, and then we start picking up those pieces as we try to rebuild the life that fell to the ground around us.

If you've ever tried to glue something that has broken, you are familiar with the fundamental rule. Two hands are needed to pick up those pieces and put them back together. When both hands are busy trying to repair your shattered life, though, how can you possibly hold onto Jesus?

We each reach a point where we have to choose between picking up those shards or grabbing on to the hem of His robe. We can't do both. We're not made that way—physically or spiritually.

There is some grief in this world that we simply cannot survive on our own. Psalm 73:26 says, "My flesh and my heart may fail, but God is the strength of my heart, my portion forever," (Holman Christian Standard Bible [HCSB]). Our flesh will fail; our hearts will fail, too. When we are faced with those soul-deep hurts that make us weep way down inside, we learn. We learn who we are to God and who He is to us.

For me, the turning point came when I was able to accept that my daughter was healed and whole...and with Jesus. My faith was a guarantee that I would see her again. Hope hadn't died with Molly's last breath. As long as I allowed my faith to grow in Jesus, He would nourish and feed hope so that it could grow in me.

The truth is, once a life is shattered, it can never be put back the way it was before. So there's no point in trying. We need to drop the pieces. Those pieces are precious. They are beautiful. They represent so much of what was good and right and blessed in our lives, and to let go of them feels like a betrayal against what—or who—we lost. Believe me, I understand. But trust me. Take it from someone who's been there and who has wrestled with God and with herself.

After all, what's the alternative? Years, maybe decades, spent trying to rebuild something that can never be put back together? Therein lies the road to endless desperation, and that's not the life my daughter would want for me. Nor is it the one my Savior died to give me.

Do it with me. Drop those jagged broken fragments of what once was and grab ahold of Jesus. Let Him do the work of rebuilding your life. He will take your pain, transforming it—and you—into something far more beautiful than you could have imagined. The process isn't quick. Neither is it easy. But as it leads you back to hope, you'll find it *is* worth it.

"The LORD is near the brokenhearted; He saves those crushed in spirit." (Psalm 34:18 HCSB)

Heather Gray

In God Alone I
Find My Home

One weekend in March, 2011 my life fell apart. After two years of giving everything to my first love, he admitted early one Saturday morning, amidst midterm week of my junior year at college, to cheating on me the previous July while I attended military training. He lied about the indiscretion for nearly a year, all the while contemplating leaving me and accusing me of being an unrighteous, jealous person, and watching me cry as I shamefully apologized for the jealous inquires and assumptions I had made about his involvement with a girl who was a friend of his. Unfortunately, my suspicions were correct because this girl turned out to be the very same girl with whom he had cheated on me. Meanwhile, I had just dropped my astrophysics major due to repeated failure and struggle with the coursework. Thus, I gave up my ambitious fourteen-year plan to achieve my dream of becoming an astronaut, and was awaiting news on whether I would be dis-enrolled from Air Force ROTC for dropping the major that had earned me a scholarship.

For the past two-and-a-half years of intense schooling and struggle, I had no loving comfort or support from my parents. I was given no sympathy, empathy, or rest. For years I had been trained to not rely on anyone—especially my family. I saw emotions as weakness and thought that in needing help with my struggles I was a burden to everyone around me. I suffered from depression and did not even know it. I contemplated ending my life ever since my junior year of high school because of the lingering depression and the constant feeling of being a burden. I had sought counseling at the university to no avail. No one cared. I failed at school, relationships, and faith. I wondered for years why God let me suffer. Although I was raised as a Catholic, I found that my family is nonetheless just as secular as ones that do not belong to a faith.

When I found out my one solid rock had just betrayed me to the greatest extent, I felt helpless, defeated, and gave up my life to God. "Do what You want. I'm just going to sit here and let the waves crash over me.

I'm done." I cracked opened the one Bible I owned and started searching for better advice than the world made available—foolish worldly advice. Words just as empty as those uttered from my parents' mouths (such as "just let it go") did nothing for me, and I swore to waste no more time contemplating this false wisdom. This worldly "wisdom" had been killing me for years and would only finish me off at this point. I figured, "Well, if this Bible thing doesn't work, then it doesn't work. But it can't hurt." After listening to me share about my hurt, good friends of mine directed me to the book of Job. For the first time in my life I truly felt that the Bible understood the realities of life. Job's friends kicked him when he was down, just like my family and close friends had been doing to me all of these years. After reading Job, returning to church, and seeking God, I found healing and happiness for the first time in my life. I had never felt so at peace before; it washed over me one day as I was just driving down the highway.

A few months later I was headed for Krasnoyarsk, Russia (in Siberia) for a summer study abroad. I couldn't wait to get out of the country and leave all the emotional wreckage and memories of the ex-boyfriend (who had moved on) behind. I was set to fly out of Boston to Dulles airport in Washington D.C. then to Moscow, Russia. Eager to get out of America, I sat anxiously aboard my plane departing from Boston, but a computer malfunction caused a two-hour delay, and airport officials at Dulles decided not to hold our connecting plane to Moscow. Stranded in D.C. waiting for my reassignment, I was miserable because of how shitty my life had been and angry at God for denying me the one thing I wanted for my twenty-first birthday the following day: to be in Moscow.

During this waiting period, I struck up conversation with the people around me. I met Kevin, a thirty-five-year-old family man from Virginia. We were stuck in line for a while and ended up chatting for two hours. I mentioned how life was pretty shitty, and how I had just been hoping to get to Moscow—to get the hell away. And he listened as I mentioned how I had been cheated on, how my father had told me afterwards, "It's okay Beck. You're not the most beautiful girl, but you're pretty, you'll find someone. Now stop talking about it and stop telling people. Just let it go." Kevin teared-up at the thought of ever doing such a thing to his daughters, and then began telling me about his past with his father and how hard he had been on him. I listened as he told me, "Everything I wanted to be happy, God gave to me. You'll be okay." I responded, "You know, everyone keeps saying I'll be okay, but I just don't believe it." He reassured me and I thought to myself: "Okay...maybe he's right". Just then a TSA agent came over and pulled Kevin out of line—he had found a connecting flight for him. We shook hands and he said he and his wife would be praying for me, and I responded I'd do the same for them. As he walked away I felt a little better having had had someone to talk to.

I faced back to the line, when I felt a tap on my shoulder: it was Kevin, with a confused look on his face. He was holding a medal and said, "This is a little weird, but I got this medal from a woman years ago in New Orleans. I had pulled out a chair for her at a restaurant and then we struck up a conversation, and she passed it on to me. I've had it for years and had totally forgotten about it, but for some reason it was on the corner of my desk this morning and something said 'Take this with you'. I think...I'm supposed to give this to you." He handed me the medal, and I said, just as confusedly, "We were supposed to meet, weren't we?" And he replied, "I think so," then went off on his way. I've never seen him again. I took the medal that instant and put it on my necklace, alongside my gold Celtic cross. One side of the medal has the image of Jesus' face on the cloth with the Latin: "God please be our light". On the other side, there is the IHS symbol, a monogram that stands for Jesus the Son, the Savior, with the Latin: "God please abide by us." It looks like it's been passed around to many people who've prayed with it and clenched it between their fingers. For the first time in my life I felt part of the larger Christian community, which then had a profound effect on me since I do not really have a family in the true sense of the word.

I went on to meet another man who had missed his flight to Argentina due to a volcanic eruption; he was also a family man. We met on the shuttle ride over to the Lansdowne Resort—where United Airlines had put me up for the night, for free, in a suite—when I had asked the four other passengers in the shuttle, "Does anyone know if a passport counts as valid ID? Because I turn twenty-one at midnight." They were all excited and that's when Scott and I started chatting. By the time we reached Lansdowne he said, "You know what, meet me at the Resort bar at midnight, and I'll buy you your first drink." Sure enough he did, and we chatted about his family and his home state of Colorado, where I had been recently. A quick hour of celebration with a complete stranger. Using Kevin and Scott, God gave me the best birthday I had ever had in my entire life. I have never forgotten that day, and realized later that if I had been in Moscow for my birthday I would not have had time to even celebrate it.

From time to time I tell people this story and there is not one person that I have told it to who has not been awe-struck by it. This experience was a huge stepping stone in my journey of faith because it was such an obvious exemplification of God's amazing love for me. He blessed me when I felt like I did not deserve it, and the blessing was so abundant. I still, absolutely, consider this moment a foundational building block in my personal relationship with God, and we've only been building higher and higher.

Two years later, I am miles and miles ahead in my walk with Christ, and I'm never looking back. I still struggle with depression, relationships, and friendships with others, but I am healing, I am being blessed each and every day by God, and He never gives up on me. That's the promise. And I definitely am a living example of its Truth.

Becky Haggerty

An Atheist's Prayer

My wife originally met Susan socially, and then she and I (along with her husband) quickly became good friends. Susan, a wife, mother and step-mother of five children, who was a well-known hard charging executive in her industry, soon become a very good client of mine as well. She seemed to have it all, well, almost. Though she came from a Christian family and married a devout Christian man, she identified herself as an atheist. Although Susan intimately knew that my Catholic faith was the center point of our life, we never talked of issues related to God or faith. Debating an atheist, and a very intelligent person, probably would have moved our relationship in the wrong direction. And I have always believed that when the time is right, God will make Himself known to those whose hearts are longing. Little did I know that our friendship would be instrumental in God's plan for Susan, as well as strengthening my own faith in the "impossible."

When Susan's son, James, was about to graduate college, he already had an engineering job lined-up. His road was seemingly set on a good path with a bright future on the horizon. One night, after going out with his college friends, he was walking home to his apartment when a drunk driver hit him full speed crossing the road. His body was thrown thirty feet into the air, landing him in a coma. When he arrived to the hospital, the doctors reported that he was technically brain-dead; and that the odds of him ever fully recovering were close to zero. For that matter, they saw a very limited possibility of him even coming out of the coma. Even in the event of a true miracle, the best doctors felt he would never be able to talk, move his body, or even feed himself. It was an unbelievable tragedy, perhaps the worst nightmare a parent could ever envision for a child.

At a loss for all hope, Susan called me. In the absence of any medical solution, she felt completely helpless and had no idea what to do. However, she remembered a few stories my wife had shared with her of our faith and our family's reliance on God's grace in times of extreme uncertainty. Without any other rational options available, Susan called me one evening to see if we could get together and pray for her son. Since she had to be at the office very early in the morning, I suggested that she come over around 6:00am before my wife and children got up.

I awoke at 5:00am to a pitch black house, where I wandered into the kitchen to begin my ten minutes of morning prayers. In the stark darkness, without any sound interrupting my focus, I prayed intensively and emotionally for James' recovery. But, I asked God for more than just a restoration back to health, I pleaded with him to make this experience something transformative for both James and his family. In other words, having always lived by the motto "Romans 8:28," I prayed that God would take this tragic event and turn it into something of an even higher meaning for the family.

After I finished praying, I quickly grabbed the remote control for the television, ready to catch the morning news as I waited for Susan's arrival. Instantly, an obscure station popped up; one that I had never seen before. My immediate thought was that one of my children had been scrolling down channels on the remote and turned off the power serendipitously on that station. As I moved my finger to type in my favorite news channel, I subconsciously paused for a moment. Without even looking at the television, I heard the word "neurosurgeon." I then looked up at the TV and noticed an interview being conducted with a famous neurosurgeon, Dr. Eben Alexander, who had taught at such renowned institutions as Harvard Medical School. Dr. Alexander had written a best-selling book entitled "Proof of Heaven: A Neurosurgeon's Journey into the Afterlife," in which he describes his near death experience in 2008. The doctor was being interviewed about his experience in order to provide some sense of hope for those surviving members of the Sandy Hook Massacre.

I was instantly captivated and continued to listen further. The doctor, who proclaimed himself as a somewhat dormant Christian, had developed a rare case of meningitis that put him into a deep coma. His brain's cortex was completely shut-down, leaving him incapable of conscious or unconscious thought (or at least how he describes his perception of the experience). Because he was a leader in his field, Dr. Alexander—having looked back at all the medical records, brain scans, and accompanying physician notes—was able to not only fully understand the gravity of his illness, but came to the same conclusion as the other attending neurosurgeons; notably, that he would never awake. And in the rare event he did, Dr. Alexander would no longer be able to talk, move, or conduct even the most basic human functions. As I closely listened to every detail, it was as if he was telling James' exact story!

Instantly I knew that this was no coincidence. I had prayed for a miracle, literally three seconds earlier, and was magically directed to a live story of how a famous neurosurgeon recovered from an almost identical fate! However, it wasn't just that he recovered, but his assertion that he spent the entire time in Heaven undergoing an experience that fundamentally changed his belief in God, our mortality, and the infinite possibilities of the Universe. He was permanently and positively transformed.

I was giddy with excitement, but unsure what any of this really meant to me, Susan or James, except the fact that this revelation was no accident. However, for several months prior, I had been having metaphysical experiences on a weekly basis—all coming in response to prayer—that led me to help others going through difficult situations. During this intense period, I believe God was giving me a tiny peak through a window—a window of His infinite possibilities—to strengthen my own faith in the absence of a rational understanding of events in our lives. Therefore, I was convinced that this, too, was a direct response to my prayers for the benefit of James and his family. I immediately left a voicemail on Susan's cell phone telling her that something unbelievable had happened, which I would explain to her once we got together. I immediately wanted to get her Dr. Alexander's book, but that would take, at least, a day even if ordered online. So I purchased the book for her on Amazon, and then printed out the synopsis, reviews, and reader feedback to get her emotions going during our prayer session.

Susan was flabbergasted with my story, and equally excited although neither of us really knew what action to take. So we prayed together that morning, and she left with a new found feeling of hope and inspiration, eagerly awaiting the delivery of Dr. Alexander's book. The next day, Susan and her husband sat at James' bedside for three days and read the book out loud. Within a day after finishing, James awoke from his coma. Then, three days later, he began to talk again. And shortly thereafter, James began to feed himself in his hospital room. To this day, the doctors have no medical explanation for his recovery. Of course, I know exactly what happened, and that was the whole point. God answered my prayers with the "perfect story" at the perfect moment, putting me in Susan's life at the time she needed His grace the most. And he put her in my life to strengthen my faith so that I would never have any doubt and be able to use that faith to help others. All things work together for good for those that love and serve the Lord.

One year later, James' recovery has been phenomenal. Though the transitions haven't been perfect and he continues to struggle with short term memory loss, his long-term memory has returned. When people meet him for the first time, there is no perceived indication that James ever suffered a brain injury. He is pleasant to be around, is active, and social. And my friend Susan no longer considers herself an atheist, but believes in God's grace and the endless possibilities He has given each of us for our limited time on Earth.

Eventually, after dozens of personal experiences like this, my metaphysical/spiritual experiences began to fade as I no longer needed "proof" of God's involvement in my life. I no longer needed to "see through that window of possibility"—and nor did I ever really—because Faith is all that is ever required.

> *"We know that in all things God works for good with those who love him, those whom he has called according to his purpose." (Romans 8:28 GNT)*

T. J. T.

5

God is Peace

"Peace. It does not mean to be in a place where there is no noise, trouble or hard work. It means to be in the midst of those things and still be calm in your heart."

– Author unknown

My Little Angel

My name is Hailey. I am a nurse, a wife, and most importantly a mother. Our first son, Jeremy, was almost sixteen months old when I found out that I was pregnant again. It was August 16, 2012. I took the pregnancy test while my husband, Brian, was at work. After receiving the results of the test, I decided to take Jeremy out to buy a "big brother" t-shirt so he could wear it when Brian walked in the door from work. Brian was surprised and very happy. Our family was growing and we were very excited for Jeremy to have a sibling.

The weekend after I found out I was pregnant, Brian and I had a thirtieth birthday/baby shower for my older sister, who was expecting in October. Even though my sister's due date was just a few months away, I couldn't resist telling my mom the news of my upcoming pregnancy. She was upstairs in her bathroom getting ready for the party. My mom was happy and hugged me, saying she wasn't that surprised! She knew something was going on with me and that we had always wanted more than one child.

The next two weeks I began to feel nauseous and tired... nothing too different than my pregnancy with Jeremy. I had started taking Pilates classes, which I really enjoyed but they were challenging and left me feeling sore some days. I assumed my tiredness and nausea were the result of overworked muscles. One day at a Pilates session around the seventh week of the pregnancy I came home, had lunch, went to the bathroom, and noticed some very light-brown spotting. I thought maybe I had over done it at Pilates. It was strange because I did not have any cramping, and I never had any sort of spotting with my first pregnancy. I called my mom, who of course assured me it wasn't a big deal and told me not to worry. I texted my sister, who said she had spotting with her daughter in the first trimester and everything turned out to be okay. I felt a bit better but was still on edge and filled with anxiety.

In my head and as a nurse, I knew that it was very common to have spotting in the beginning of a pregnancy. I needed to wait and keep an eye on the bleeding. But in my heart I just knew that something wasn't right.

I never even put the thought of a miscarriage in my head. After all, no one in my family had had one—not my sister, not my mother. I decided that I would keep an eye on the spotting and not jump the gun calling my doctor.

It was the same the next day: not there every time I wiped, but on and off and never very much. I decided to call the doctor. Of course she said it was common and that if it changed to red, or the amount increased, or if I felt any cramps I should call back. That weekend I went to work at the hospital and the spotting actually went away. I felt some relief and thought that maybe things were going to be okay.

The next week, my eighth week of pregnancy, the spotting started again. This time it was not brown anymore… it was a dark red. Again it wasn't very much, so I fought the urge to call the doctor as my first prenatal appointment was to be at nine weeks. As the week went on, the amount of the spotting picked up a little but still wasn't very much. I decided to call because it was a deep red now, and I noticed a smell. The smell was kind of what freaked me out. It reminded me of what the blood smelled like after I had Jeremy. I can't describe it, and maybe this is the nurse in me talking, but it really had me worried. This was Friday, and my appointment was for Monday, but my doctor said I could come in at noon anyways.

Brian was at work, and my mom was able to help me with Jeremy, so I did not have to take him with me. I dropped him off at my parents and arrived at the doctor. I had to wait forty-five minutes to be seen—the longest forty-five minutes of my life. I ran into a friend from high school who also sees the same doctor and was pregnant, too. It was very uncomfortable trying to decide what to tell her, but I ended up saying I was pregnant and that this was my first appointment. She was happy for me. Little did she know that on the inside I was a ball of nerves and just wanted to get back and see the doctor and make sure my baby was okay.

Finally, it was my turn. I went in the first room on the left—the same room I first saw Jeremy as a tiny bean on the ultrasound machine. My doctor came in and asked a few questions. She didn't waste any time and got the ultrasound machine ready. Right away she saw the dark red blood; she turned the screen away from me so that I could not see it. I knew right then what I had already known in my heart. There was no heartbeat… there was no baby. She used the term blighted ovum. She hugged me, said she was sorry and gave me a tissue. I cried a little and was still in shock. I really wished Brian was with me.

The doctor said that I needed to go have my blood drawn so she could see read my HCG levels. The diagnosis on the blood-work order form is a term I will never forget: "missed abortion." I remember thinking, "abortion?" How can that be? I didn't choose this. I would never have an abortion! Why is that even a term used for someone who loses a baby? I knew it was medical terminology, but it stung so bad to see it written out. I left the exam room trying my best to keep my lips from quivering. I made it out the door and just started crying. By the time I made it to my car, questions ran through my mind. Why was this happening? I would never see or hold this sweet little baby. I still felt nauseous—maybe the baby would be okay, and I would still be pregnant. What if this was a little girl—I wanted a daughter so badly. Nobody in my immediate family had miscarried, why me? Jeremy was going to be such a good big brother. So sad.

I went to the lab and had the blood work completed. My levels were high and equivalent to someone who was around nine weeks pregnant. My doctor was surprised with the results when she called. Based on what she saw she was not expecting my levels to be that high. She said that if I did not begin bleeding more and passing the baby naturally, I would need to have a D&C, which is when you have to go and have the baby and sac surgically removed from your uterus. Great, after all this I may need surgery? Why was this happening?

That weekend was one of the hardest weekends of my life. I was hosting one of my best friend's bridal shower, and I was miscarrying my sweet baby. I put on my happy face but physically was in pain and emotionally was devastated. The bleeding and cramping picked up big time, and by Monday, September 24, 2012, I miscarried the baby. I had to continue having my blood checked to make sure my levels returned to normal. I had to continue taking pregnancy tests and reporting to my doctor until they became negative, which took weeks. It was terrible. I was so sad. Nobody knows what to say, and the things they do say only make it worse. Especially "at least it was early on" or "God has a plan, you'll have more children." I wanted that child. Why would God's plan include so much sadness and pain? I found comfort and understanding in talking with my mother-in-law, who also miscarried a baby around six weeks.

As time has passed, I definitely feel more peace and comfort about the baby I lost. We were blessed with another son on July 31, 2013. Through prayer, my husband, my sweet sons, and my family the pain has lessened. Reflecting on this time will always make me sad, but I know that one day I will get to see my baby in heaven.

I have learned one huge lesson: ultimately, that we are not in charge. Everything does happen for a reason, and we don't always know what that reason is. God knows our path long before we walk it. God's timing is perfect and does not always coincide with our timing. By keeping faith in His wisdom and knowing that He is only a loving God, we can fulfill His will for our life. I will always think about my little angel and what could have been. But, I will also rest easy knowing that he or she is perfect and with God. He or she never had to feel pain or know the imperfection here on earth.

Hailey Fuhr

Miracles are Made in Heaven

Life is a miracle. I believe this to be true with all of my heart because through many difficulties in my life I have also been blessed with miraculous experiences. The youngest of ten children, I was born with congenital dysplasia of the hip (CDH) and officially diagnosed at twenty-months-of-age. The diagnosis gave my parents the much needed answers for my unusual struggle with mobility.

Following the diagnosis, I underwent surgery to re-position my hips, which left my fragile little body in restrictive castings for a total of forty months. During this time, the doctors told my parents that there was a ninety percent chance I would never walk. Well, my mother refused to accept this as my future, so she prayed that one day I would have a different outcome than what the doctor stated could occur. My mother had great faith and though my father always went to Mass, it was she who instilled in us kids that faith is an important part of daily life. Miraculously, after years of immobility, my mother's prayers were answered and, at seven years-of-age, I took my first steps. This milestone proved to be just one of many physical feats within my life.

The years of new-found walking likely placed weight-bearing stress on my hips because by the age of sixteen, the ball in one of my hips had turned around. This unwelcomed re-positioning of my hip required another surgical procedure for repair. I was placed in a body cast for the fifth time of my young life. Following the surgery, I was sent to Children's Seashore House in Atlantic City, New Jersey, where I undertook the daunting task of learning to walk all over again.

In 1985, approximately twenty-four years later, my husband and I were living in California, where we owned a hoagie shop. One day, when I turned to get some tomatoes from the refrigerator, both of my hips gave-out. I was unable to go to the hospital because we did not have health insurance at the time. In desperate need of medical attention, I sought care at a walk-in clinic, where I was merely placed on crutches. The respective medical staff told me that I would not be able to walk on my own again until I received double-hip-replacement surgery. Unfortunately, due to my lack of health insurance, I had no choice but to remain on the crutches for the next four years until I was finally able to undergo the first of my hip-replacement surgeries.

During the recovery of my right hip-replacement, I was dropped by a physical therapist in the hall of the hospital. X-ray results revealed no damage had been done to my new right hip, but the tremendous swelling of my leg indicated otherwise. Consequently, I sought treatment through four months of physical therapy. However, when my leg showed no sign of improvement following the therapy, I was scheduled for an electromyogram (EMG) test. The results of the test showed I suffered nerve damage from the fall in the hospital. Fortunately, a mere six months later my nerves regenerated, leading to the recovery of my leg.

After experiencing the unfortunate mishap of being dropped in the hospital, many people wondered why I did not sue. My response to their questions was that I did not see the need to do so because mistakes happen; no one is perfect. Throughout this troubling experience, I prayed to God asking only two things: (1) that I would be able to walk again, and (2) that I would be able to work so I could pay my bills. God graciously answered both of my prayers, so why would I ask for anything more than I needed?

Well, as life would have it, my trials continued. In 1986, I underwent a total left-hip-replacement surgery. The surgery, scheduled at 1:00pm, was supposed to take only four hours to complete. But I knew something went wrong when I woke-up in the operating room almost seven hours later. Apparently, the new hip had been mistakenly sent to a sister hospital, instead of the hospital where I was a registered patient, due to miscommunication between the hospital staff and the courier. Thankfully, the hip had arrived at the correct hospital just in the knick-of-time, enabling a successful surgery without posing any further complications. Amazingly, I was in great condition following the surgery and did not need to undergo physical therapy. I attribute this speedy recovery to all the people who were praying for me.

Later that year, I was informed by my doctor that I needed to have both of my knees replaced. The doctor had said that whenever there are hip problems, the person has to rely on the knees for most of the walking to compensate where the hips are lacking in mobility, so the knees typically have to be replaced. When I received this news, I was not mentally or physically prepared to undergo yet another two surgeries in such a short period of time following my hip replacements. Therefore, I postponed the surgeries until May of 2003. Once I had the knee surgeries performed, I was told I would eventually need a second left hip replacement.

Six months following my knee surgeries, I broke my wrist and was in a cast for about a month-and-a-half. The cast was removed the day after Christmas of that year. On that following Monday, December 29, I was involved in a head-on car accident that left me severely injured with a punctured and collapsed lung, two crushed femur bones, and numerous broken bones that included my wrist (the very same wrist that had just healed from the previous break), four ribs, and my knee that had just been replaced.

I was rushed by ambulance to the hospital. Since I was in critical condition, my brother and sisters who lived in the area came to see me as soon as they received the news of my accident. My state of health was so poor that I was lingering at death's doorstep. During this fragile moment in time, my husband John took the reins of the situation and steered me to safety. He persistently advocated for the aggressive treatment of my health by challenging the doctors to think outside of the box.

By the divine intervention of John's guardian angel, he had the audacity to tell the doctor to transfer me to an out-of-state hospital since the doctors at the other hospital already knew my background with the two knee surgeries. At the time, the doctor did not agree with John's request because he believed it would be too large of a risk to move me in such a critical state of health. In short, the doctor did not think I would survive the travel. Despite the doctor's warnings, John felt strongly about my need to be transferred and did not back down with his request until it was finally decided that I would be moved by helicopter to the other hospital.

When we arrived at the second hospital, the attending doctor told John that the physician from the first hospital had informed him of my critical condition. Based on my state of health upon arrival, the attending doctor told my husband that he would have to put me in a self-induced coma for twenty-four hours in order to relax my body so he could operate on me the following day.

After the nine-and-a-half operation was performed, I was kept in intensive care for ten days and placed on a ventilator; the doctors did not expect me to live due to the severity of my condition. I remained in the hospital for thirty more days until I was given the unanticipated allowance to go home on February 6, 2004. John's keen presence of mind during the most critical point of my suffering saved my life. God undoubtedly blessed me through my spouse.

Although I had been released from the hospital, I was still unable to move on my own. I was forced to learn how to slide on a board to get from my bed into the wheel chair, and vice versa. I continued to get around in this manner until my appointment one month later on St. Patrick's Day. I prayed to St. Patrick for help with my mobility, and once again my prayers were answered. Despite all the physical injuries my body had suffered, the Lord was merciful. He granted me the healing that enabled me to not only pull-through but to get-up and walk once again.

Though life was good, it still posed its challenges. A couple of years later, I discovered that my left femur bone did not heal correctly from its injury sustained during the car accident. At this point, I thought to myself, *what's one more surgery?* So in April 2005, I underwent a four-and-a-half-hour operation to have over one hundred pieces of screws, nuts, bolts and rods inserted into my femur bone as well as to replace my left hip for the second time.

On the evening of October 23, 2010, John and I were driving in our car when we were hit by another driver; our car was totaled. The crash smashed the trunk of our car into the back seat, and the gas tank was found on the ground. Thankfully our tank was nearly empty, otherwise it would have exploded. My husband and I were lucky, to say the least, but I did not walk away from the accident scot-free. My left shoulder was injured in the crash, which required a total shoulder replacement, sending me back to physical therapy just one year after my knee and second left hip surgeries. Eight months after the shoulder replacement surgery, I was left with only half the use of my left shoulder, but I am fine with that. I have come to realize that I can deal with anything that life hands me because God is with me through it all.

Almost one year later, on September 30, 2011, some discomfort manifested in my chest. Unsure of what was causing the pain, I visited a walk-in clinic to have my symptoms checked out. I was told that the discomfort was likely caused by reflux and advised to take some over-the-counter medication to ease the pain. Well, the pain continued for thirty more hours, but because I attributed the chest pain to either something I had eaten or anxiety, I didn't do much else about it. Consequently, the pain did not subside. I ended up sitting in a chair all night because the pain in my chest prevented me from comfortably lying down.

The next day, a friend of mine called to ask me to make five phone-calls on behalf of the St. Vincent de Paul Society, which I often did. I told her that I was unable to make the calls because the pain in my chest was unbearable. She immediately urged me to call 911, but I didn't think my pain was emergency-worthy. Alarmed at my lack of urgency in the matter, she told me that if I didn't make the call, then she would. Since I thought it would be ridiculous for her to call 911 and not me, I reluctantly requested emergency help.

Within forty-five minutes I was in the emergency room (ER) with a code blue: I had a blocked right coronary artery that required the immediate surgical insertion of two stents. During my hospital stay I was told that eighty percent of women die from heart disease because, like me, they often do not recognize the signs of a heart attack. The nurse told me, for future reference, that if the chest pain is not relieved after taking two Tums, then I need to call 911.

Miraculously, by the grace of God, I was sent home the very next day after receiving heart surgery. Sadly, one of my brothers died from a heart attack at the young age of fifty-five. I count my blessings that I did not suffer the same fate, and I am forever thankful that my friend called me that day. Her phone call saved my life.

Well, if you would believe it, I fell and broke my wrist for the third time, in October of 2012. After I called my friends and family informing them about my latest injury, a friend of mine said to her husband, "This woman has been through so much, how does she find the strength to survive?"

In response to her question, I just have to say that I find my strength through prayer. God handles everything for us if we allow Him. It is truly the power of prayer that has gotten me through all the pain and physical set-backs that I have suffered throughout my life. I could have easily blamed God for all of it, but I refuse to because, despite all of the struggles I have faced, God has always been there to pull me safely through. So instead of allowing self-pity to set in, I focus on the positive in life: my heart is still beating, my smile is gleaming, and God loves me. At the beautiful age of sixty-seven, I understand that life truly is a miracle, and I am forever grateful that God has blessed me with so many years to live it.

Sally Drane Dellaquila

The Picture

When my sister, Rosie, first told us she had Leukemia, I researched all I could about it and learned that the last attempt for patient recovery is a bone marrow transplant. I told my sister right then that I would be a donor for her. After all, my whole life I have been told that I look just like her, so I naturally thought our blood would be a perfect match.

Rosie lived in Oklahoma at the time while I lived in Pennsylvania, so I had to fly to Oklahoma for the doctors to harvest my marrow. After the transplant was performed, I received updates from the family; some were encouraging while others were scary. I never heard if the transplant was working; the doctors said it could take up to four weeks to tell. And then, almost four weeks to the day of the transplant, my sister lost her battle. When one of my brothers-in-law called to tell me, I was devastated. I felt like a failure. One of my other sisters was also a match, but doctors chose me for the transplant because I was younger by ten years. I couldn't help but wonder if the outcome would have been different if my sister had been the donor instead of me.

I felt like my family wouldn't want me to come home for the funeral because I didn't make Rosie better. I thought she didn't make it because my bone marrow wasn't good enough. I was so crushed. I would not take their calls because I just could not bear to hear their disappointment in the fact that my marrow did not save our sister. However, my husband and children were very supportive and encouraged me to go to the funeral anyways; thanks to them, I got on a plane to Oklahoma.

When my niece found out that I felt like it was my fault Rosie didn't survive, she took me aside and told me that all of the markers had shown up to indicate she could have survived had her lungs and chest not become infected.

My beautiful sister passed away in June of 2012. Her birthday was the next month, July 23rd; she would have been sixty-nine years old. I dreaded that Monday and was not sure how I would do at work on her birthday, just a month after her passing.

I have to shift gears here to explain something else. I turned fifty in April of 2011 and, while home for a visit with my family in Oklahoma, they held a surprise birthday party for me at my old church, St. Clement in Bixby. A picture was taken on the altar of that church of me with four of my eight sisters, Rosie being one of them. Shortly after I returned to Pennsylvania I opened that picture on my home computer and tried to e-mail it to my work e-mail unsuccessfully. In mid-April of 2011 it must have gotten stuck in cyber-space because we had moved and changed internet suppliers a few times; our e-mail got changed, but the Outlook program stayed attached to a disconnected account. Anyway, my husband had worked on our computer unbeknownst to me the weekend right before Rosie's birthday. He got our Outlook connected to our new e-mail, which released some e-mails.

On July 23, 2012 when I arrived at work and got my computer up and running the first thing I saw were four e-mails from our old e-mail account with pictures attached. The first or second one I opened was the one of my sisters and me on the altar at St. Clement. My sister who had passed away stood just to my right in the picture. I didn't cry that day, and I haven't felt like crying for Rosie since. I feel like the Lord is comforting me with a picture that was lost in cyber-space for over fifteen months and just happened to show up on, of all days, her birthday.

Lisa Bruce

Reunited in Faith

In 1988, I was a member of an ethnically diverse Roman Catholic Church in Woodside, Queens, and was a Eucharistic Minister. I became friendly with a couple who were fellow parishioners. The woman served the church as a lector, and her husband was also a Eucharistic Minister. Because of a chronic health condition, the woman had to retire early from her teaching position, but her husband continued to work as an accountant for the New York City Transit Authority.

As our friendship developed, the three of us enjoyed dining at the neighborhood's Italian and Chinese restaurants. Frequently as I got off the subway after work, I would meet the couple walking their beloved German shepherd, "Schatzi", and we would engage in lively conversations. On one memorable evening, my boyfriend and I joined my friends to attend a concert featuring Dennis Day, the Irish singer from the "Jack Benny Show". After the concert the four of us adjourned to a nearby pub, hoisted a few pints and sang Irish songs.

Unexpectedly, I discovered a reasonably priced one-bedroom co-op apartment in another section of Queens and moved away. I joined a nearby Catholic Church and again served as a Eucharistic Minister. My friendship with the couple continued. I hosted a dinner for them at my new apartment. There were shared Christmas and birthday celebrations.

But, as so often happens in life, our get-togethers became less frequent. I began taking evening courses in business administration at La Guardia Community College. Working every day and burdened with homework, my contacts with the couple were mostly by phone. I knew the husband was nearing retirement age, and they were considering moving out of state. Then, one Christmas I sent a card with a long letter, and the mail was returned with the notation, "Moved, No Forwarding Address". I was stunned at the abrupt end of a long friendship.

September 11, 2001, affected so many New Yorkers. The morning after this horrible disaster, I stood on the platform of the Woodside, Queens, subway station and looked across at the Manhattan skyline. Where there had been two high buildings, there was just a dense cloud of smoke. I cried and prayed for the three-thousand people who had perished the day before. I thanked God, too. No one in my family or any of my friends had been killed.

Fearful of the devastation which happened to many businesses in the Wall Street area, the CEO of the publishing company where I was employed announced the financial division was moving out of the city. Since I was a billing supervisor in this division, my life was about to change. For a year rumors spread fast and furious. The division was being relocated to Virginia? Vermont? Connecticut? Pennsylvania? Finally, the new location was revealed—Wilmington, Delaware! Oh, yes, I drove through Delaware once on my way to Washington, D.C.

I had a critical decision to make: stay in New York and look for another job at the age of sixty-two or move to Delaware and work three more years until retirement age. The publishing company offered a generous relocation package: 1.) Increase in salary, 2.) a twenty-five percent bonus, and 3.) the services of a real-estate broker to find another home.

Wilmington, Delaware, became my home in February 2003. Talk about feeling lost! It was as though I had landed in a foreign country. From a city with a population of four million, I had moved to a city with just seventy thousand. Except for my boss and two other relocated New Yorkers, I did not know a soul. There were no subways. Bus transportation was limited. No newsstands. No all-night delicatessens. The downtown area was deserted after 5:15pm.

For six months, I wandered around in a daze. A neighbor in my condominium association had recommended a Catholic Church within walking distance. I began to attend daily Mass. The friendly pastor introduced me to other parishioners and I began to finally feel at home.

The Sunday Bulletin made an appeal for additional lectors and Eucharistic Ministers, and I was formally installed as a Eucharistic Minister in my new parish. On the recommendation of my pastor, I joined the Pastoral Care Department of St. Francis Hospital. There I visited all the Catholic patients and brought them the Holy Eucharist. I prayed with patients who were about to undergo cancer surgery. I toured the maternity ward and saw mothers nursing their newborns. I gave each baby a blessed Miraculous Medal.

When I arrived at the hospice unit one morning, the head nurse informed me an elderly woman patient had died ten minutes earlier. Unfortunately, the hospital chaplain had not yet arrived at the hospital. Would I pray with the family? I entered the patient's room and was greeted by a family of seven members: her eighty-five-year-old husband, four adult children and two teenage grandchildren. The "Our Father" was recited, and each family member received the Blessed Sacrament of Our Lord. Then, we hugged and kissed each other. Truly, it was an emotional and spiritual experience.

One morning in January 2014, I was on my rounds on the seventh floor. Outside of the last room, I looked at the patient's name on the chart. It was a very unusual woman's name. It was the same name as the friend I knew twenty-five-years-ago in Queens. I thought, "Oh, this must be a relative of my former friend." When I entered the room, I discovered it was, indeed, my long lost friend!

After recovering from our mutual surprise, my friend received the Holy Eucharist. I finished my rounds and returned to her room. She was quite weak so our conversation was brief. However, I learned she had moved from New Jersey to Wilmington in 1999 after her husband had died to be near two women cousins—her only relatives. She resided in an assisted living complex only two blocks from my condominium. In that period of time, we had never met—not in the park, not in the nearby supermarket and not in church!

Shortly after our reunion, my friend moved to a nursing home. When I called, I was informed she was not strong enough to have visitors. So over the ensuing weeks, we visited on the telephone. We chatted about the different personal events that had occurred over the ensuing years. Less than a year after their move to New Jersey, her husband had died from a sudden heart attack. For five years, my mother had suffered from cancer of the esophagus, and when she died, her passing left me extremely bereft. Yet, our personal losses strengthened our faith in the loving heart of Jesus, who is the true Savior of the world. Frequent attendance at Mass and prayers to Him and His Beloved Mother rekindled our shared belief in an everlasting life.

Because my friend loved animals and was devoted to St. Francis of Assisi she had joined the Third Order of St. Francis. I described my trip to Assisi and the visit to the tomb of St. Francis. On another occasion, the Shrine of Our Lady of Lourdes became the topic of our conversation. I had traveled to Lourdes in 2001 with other members of my then Queens parish. Seeing the candlelight procession of the sick to Our Lady's Grotto, and sharing the memory with my friend, was quite a poignant experience.

Every time I telephoned her voice seemed to get weaker and weaker. Finally, I called one of her cousins who said my friend was in the final stages of lung cancer. Each week a priest from St. Hedwig's Catholic Church brought my friend the Holy Eucharist. Sadly, the last time I saw my friend was at her Funeral Mass, but I was happy to be able to say a fond goodbye and firmly believe she and her husband are now with Our Blessed Lord in heaven.

Margaret Kenney

My Mother's Journey to Heaven

My mother, Lucia, or "Lucy" as she was known, was a compassionate, loving and energetic person. She was an exceptional wife to my father for fifty-five-and-a-half-years, an inspirational and devoted mother to her three children, and an incredible Mom-Mom to her six grandchildren. She lived a Christian life and was always smiling. My mother and I were very close and I would like to elaborate on the final two years of her life. You will come to see what a remarkable woman she was.

On a Friday in early November, 2001, my mother had her yearly appointment with her family doctor. That night, my husband, Joe, and I decided to go out to dinner and just as we were finishing our meal, my cell phone rang. My brother had called to inform us that our mother was admitted to the hospital after her doctor's appointment. Since my brother did not inform me why she had been admitted, my husband and I drove directly to the hospital, which was located on the other side of town. During the drive to the hospital, my imagination was running wild and I feared the worst.

When we arrived at the hospital, we were met by my dad, brother and sister. My mother was in her bed talking to a nurse. As I scanned the room, trying to comprehend what was actually happening, I noticed a brochure entitled, "Oncology" placed on her bedside table. I instantly knew something was terribly wrong. The nurse informed my mother that tests would be conducted over the weekend, and to our surprise, she took the news very well. My mother had an incredible faith.

The next morning, I received a call from my mother informing me that the doctor decided to have her return to the hospital for the tests later that week so she was being discharged. I immediately telephoned my father to give him the news and we drove together to bring her back home. My husband and I, along with our son Brian, lived around the corner from my parent's home so we were able to visit them practically every day. We always enjoyed our conversations and especially "our cup of coffee" with them. How we miss those days!

When all the tests were completed, my mother, along with the rest of us, was advised that she had ovarian cancer. We were stunned, to say the least, and very, very sad. We could only pray for her and give her all of our support.

Two days before Thanksgiving, an operation to remove the tumors from her body was scheduled. After the surgery, the surgeon sadly informed us that she was in Stage Three of the cancer, the second to the last stage of the disease. Without chemotherapy, she would probably have only one year left to live. After receiving this news, it seemed like my whole world was falling apart, but I found comfort knowing that we both had a strong faith and that somehow, we would get through this ordeal. So, I constantly prayed for my mother and her condition.

My mother began her first chemotherapy treatment the day after her seventy-fourth birthday, which was the feast day of St. Lucy—thus the reason "Lucia" was chosen as her name. Overall, she had a total of six treatments. Each treatment left her with a lasting pain for a few days. I believe she drew strength and comfort by praying the rosary, which she prayed every night. She also felt the continued love and care from her family each day.

Within weeks of her final chemotherapy treatment, my son, Brian, was graduating from Johns Hopkins University in May, 2002. With her strength beginning to slowly return, she felt able enough to attend the commencement. My mother not only bought a beautiful dress for Brian's graduation, but she also bought a new wig (her hair was slowly growing back). She was so excited to be traveling to Baltimore, Maryland for his graduation because she would have the opportunity to see her grandson receive a degree in physics. Having her attend his graduation was a day we will always remember!

As my mother's health began to improve steadily, she insisted to continue with her daily tasks at home, though she was not able to do as much as she used to and I made sure to assist her every day. My place of employment was conveniently located across the street from my home, so after work, I would go directly to my parent's home to visit for an hour or two.

Then, to our dismay, we received news in January, 2003 that more tumors had returned and there was nothing more that could be done for my mother. The final days we so dreadfully anticipated had arrived.

Soon after this news, the doctor placed my mother under hospice care, and on Valentine's Day, two nurses arrived at her home to complete the paperwork. Twice a week the nurse would visit and perform her duties while the hospice aide would sponge bathe my mother every Monday, Wednesday and Friday. In the midst of their duties, they would take the time to chat with us, knowing that the conversation was something my mother looked forward to, despite the circumstances. The nurse and aide always enjoyed their visits and showed so much compassion towards my mother.

To help our parents when the hospice nurse and aide were not present, my brother, sister and I decided that we would take turns staying overnight every week to make sure our mother had everything she needed and was comfortable. This assistance also allowed our father to rest in the evenings.

On March 20, 2003, my mother became permanently bedridden, and we became more and more concerned as her condition was deteriorating. But, she always kept a positive attitude throughout her illness. Many times, she would say, "I have to accept what God sends to me." Never once did I hear my mother ask God why this was happening to her! By Easter, the hospice nurse told us that my mother only had a matter of time. I could not bear to hear such news and became more anxious with each passing day.

The Friday before she passed away, a hospital bed was delivered to her home. Prior to this, she had remained in her own bed, which was conveniently set-up in her dining room. As soon as she was given the remote control to the hospital bed, she began to push the "up" and "down" buttons. She kept pushing the "up" button for the foot of the bed so many times, that it started to make a grinding noise. When asked where she thought she was going by pushing the button, she didn't hesitate and responded, "Up to Heaven."

Sadly enough, my mother passed away on the following Monday, April 28, 2003. I had prayed that I would be by her side when she took her last breath—God answered my prayers. I was at her bedside from noon the preceding day until her passing at approximately 8:30pm. I am so grateful to God that He allowed me to be with my mother when she left this earth to make her "Journey to Heaven".

Her wake and funeral were held on May 5, 2003. Since Mother's Day was on May 11th of that year, I bought an artificial flower and pinned it on her dress during the wake. My mother's funeral Mass was held at our parish church. During the Mass, five of her grandchildren carried the "Gifts" (the Host and Chalice) to the priest. My son delivered a beautiful eulogy to his grandmother after the Mass. Since I had prepared her funeral Mass, I thought it would be appropriate to have "Santa Lucia" sung as we processed out of church.

A few weeks after my mother's funeral, I had a dream that brought some peace to my heart. In the dream, I was in the backseat of a car and my mother was sitting in the front seat. When she turned around to look at me, I said, "Oh, Mom, I had them sing, 'Santa Lucia', at your funeral Mass." She answered, "I know. Thank you." The dream was so vivid and I knew from that time on, she would always be with me. Since her passing, there has not been a day that has gone by that I don't either hear or see her name. I have received many signs over the past several years, letting me know that she is in Heaven and watching over me.

Though I miss my mother tremendously, I am comforted that she is now in God's presence. No longer will she experience sadness and pain but rather eternal happiness and love. God blessed me with a beautiful woman, both inside and out, as a mother. She was a wonderful role model to not only me but also to her grandchildren. Whenever I see someone who knew her, the first thing they recall is the smile she always had on her face. Her name truly fit her personality: "Lucia," which in Italian means "Light". She was the "bright light' of our family! May she rest in eternal peace.

Anne M. (De Rocili) Smigielski

Safely Home

Before my mother-in-law died, I asked her to please give me a sign (after she died) that she was in heaven. She said she would try. She also wondered how I could be sure it was a true spiritual sign and not something merely interpreted by me. I said, "Just make sure I know it's from you and that I will have no doubt that you are in heaven." Again, she said she would do her best.

The day before I was leaving to see my son Michael, I told my husband Johnny I wanted to go to the local Christian book store to buy Michael an inspirational present that he could take with him on his deployment to the Persian Gulf. I went to the store and began looking, but could not find the right thing. So, I said a prayer and asked the Lord to please guide me toward something that would be right for Michael. As I turned and looked down, I saw a prayer card with Jesus holding a lamb in his arms. I turned it over and saw the title "Safely Home". *Yes,* I thought, *this may be the right thing because I sure want Michael to return safely home.* As I began reading, however, it quickly became apparent based on *the wording of this prayer,* that there was *no doubt* this card was a message from my mother-in-law. The following excerpt from the poetic prayer, "Safely Home", spoke directly to my heart:

> I am home in Heaven, dear ones;
> Oh, so happy and so bright!
> There is perfect joy and beauty
> In this everlasting light.
>
> All the pain and grief is over,
> Every restless tossing passed;
> I am now at peace forever,
> Safely home in Heaven, at last. (1-8, Anonymous)

As tears were streaming down my face, I went to the register and asked if they had any more prayer cards like this one. Two people checked. They did not have any others like this card in the entire store...

I believe in my heart that my mother-in-law wants the family to know that she is truly "Safely Home".

K. A. R.

Closing Remarks

Dear Reader,

This book was created to share God's love and mercy with *you* through the documentation of true accounts of the beauty, hope and love that people have witnessed and received by opening their hearts to God and inviting Him into their lives.

With this in mind, I hope the stories in this book can do for you the same that they have done for me: provide a simple, yet inspiring, way for learning and growing in the love that God, our Lord, has gifted us. Whatever you have or will experience in your life, my hope and prayer is that you will open your heart to receive the mercy, peace and love that God has ready for you. He is very much alive in every one of us. He is the Truth. He is the Way.

May God bless you and keep you all the days of your life.

Yours in Christ,
Jacquelyn Scott, MHP

Be at Peace
Prayer by St. Francis de Sales

Do not look forward in fear to the changes in life;
rather, look to them with full hope as they arise,
God, whose very own you are,
will lead you safely through all things;
and when you cannot stand it,
God will carry you in His arms.
Do not fear what may happen tomorrow;
the same understanding Father who cares for you today
will take care of you then and every day.
He will either shield you from suffering
or will give you unfailing strength to bear it.
Be at peace,
and put aside all anxious thoughts and imaginations.
Amen.

About the Author

Jacquelyn Scott, MHP is a stay-at-home mother who, like many, faces the daily challenge of balancing multiple roles, such as spouse, parent, and individual. Prior to the birth of her children, Jacquelyn was largely involved with the University of Delaware where she obtained a Master of Science degree in Health Promotion. Through her studies she found that optimal quality of life is achieved through the balance of physical, emotional, social, mental, and *spiritual* health.

Graduate school further opened the door to Jacquelyn's passion for writing to expand upon her interest in spirituality's influence on quality of life. Jacquelyn understands that placing one's trust in God is essential for successfully navigating the everyday norms and unexpected hardships, and she strives to share God's love with others through her writing.

Jacquelyn's faith-inspired poem, "Engulfed", was published in the poetry anthology *From a Window: Equality* by Eber & Wein Publishing. She has also authored several articles for Examiner.com as the Wilmington Faith & Empowerment Examiner.

Jacquelyn and her husband, Brad, live in Newark, Delaware with their three children. She can be reached at inspirationalbook.jrs@gmail.com.